Reality Beyond the Veil

*Revealing the True Nature of Reality
with Quantum Conciseness*

Sai Venkatram

Copyright © 2023 Sai Venkatram

All rights reserved

The characters and events portrayed in this book are fictitious. Any similarity to real persons, living or dead, is coincidental and not intended by the author.

No part of this book may be reproduced, or stored in a retrieval system, or transmitted in any form or by any means, electronic, mechanical, photocopying, recording, or otherwise, without express written permission of the publisher.

"Reality is merely an illusion, albeit a very persistent one." - Albert Einstein

CONTENTS

Title Page
Copyright
Epigraph
Preface
Introduction
Prologue
Foreword

Chapter 1: Introduction	1
Chapter 1.1: What is Quantum Consciousness?	3
Chapter 1.2: The History of Quantum Consciousness	5
Chapter 1.3: Why Quantum Consciousness Matters	7
Chapter 2: Quantum Mechanics Basics	9
Chapter 2.1: The Double-Slit Experiment	11
Chapter 2.2: Wave-Particle Duality	14
Chapter 2.3: Quantum Entanglement	16
Chapter 3: The Brain and Consciousness	18
Chapter 3.1: The Neurobiological Basis of Consciousness	21
Chapter 3.2: The Hard Problem of Consciousness	23
Chapter 3.3: The Integrated Information Theory of Consciousness	26
Chapter 4: Quantum Information Theory	29
Chapter 4.1: Quantum Bits (Qubits)	32

Chapter 4.2: Quantum Gates	35
Chapter 4.3: Quantum Algorithms	38
Chapter 5: Quantum Computers and Consciousness	41
Chapter 5.1: The Potential of Quantum Computing for Consciousness Studies	44
Chapter 5.2: The Challenges of Building a Quantum Computer for Consciousness Studies	46
Chapter 5.3: The Future of Quantum Computing and Consciousness Studies	48
Chapter 6: The Quantum Zeno Effect	50
6.1: Definition of the Quantum Zeno Effect	52
Chapter 6.2: The Quantum Zeno Effect and Consciousness	54
Chapter 6.3: Experimental Evidence for the Quantum Zeno Effect	56
Chapter 7: Quantum Mechanics and the Mind-Body Problem	58
Chapter 7.1: The Mind-Body Problem and its History	62
Chapter 7.2: How Quantum Mechanics Can Help Solve the Mind-Body Problem	65
Chapter 7.3: Objections to Quantum Mechanics as a Solution to the Mind-Body Problem	67
Chapter 8: Quantum Nonlocality and Consciousness	69
Chapter 8.1: Definition of Nonlocality	71
Chapter 8.2: The Role of Nonlocality in Consciousness	73
Chapter 8.3: Experimental Evidence for Quantum Nonlocality	75
Chapter 9: Quantum Biology	79
Chapter 9.1: The Emergence of Quantum Biology	84
Chapter 9.2: Quantum Biology and Consciousness	88
Chapter 9.3: The Future of Quantum Biology and	91

Consciousness Studies

Chapter 10: Quantum Information Processing in the Brain	94
Chapter 10.1: The Role of Quantum Information Processing in the Brain	99
Chapter 10.2: Experimental Evidence for Quantum Information Processing in the Brain	104
Chapter 10.3: The Implications of Quantum Information Processing for Consciousness	109
Chapter 11: Quantum Field Theory and Consciousness	112
Chapter 11.1: Definition of Quantum Field Theory	116
Chapter 11.2: The Role of Quantum Field Theory in Consciousness	118
Chapter 11.3: Experimental Evidence for Quantum Field Theory and Consciousness	122
Chapter 12: Quantum Mechanics and the Nature of Reality	126
Chapter 12.1: The Copenhagen Interpretation of Quantum Mechanics	131
Chapter 12.2: The Many-Worlds Interpretation of Quantum Mechanics	135
Chapter 12.3: Implications of Quantum Mechanics for the Nature of Reality and Consciousness	138
Chapter 13: Quantum Consciousness and Mysticism	142
Chapter 13.1: The Connection Between Quantum Consciousness and Mysticism	146
Chapter 13.2: The Implications of Quantum Consciousness for Spirituality	151
Chapter 13.3: Criticisms of the Connection Between Quantum Consciousness and Mysticism	155
Chapter 14: Quantum Consciousness and Artificial Intelligence	158

Chapter 14.1: The Role of Quantum Consciousness in Artificial Intelligence	161
Chapter 14.2: The Potential Benefits of Integrating Quantum Consciousness into AI	168
Chapter 14.3: The Ethical Implications of Quantum Consciousness in AI	171
Chapter 15: Quantum Mechanics and Free Will	174
Chapter 15.1: The Definition of Free Will	178
Chapter 15.2: The Role of Quantum Mechanics in Free Will	179
Chapter 15.3: Criticisms of the Connection Between Quantum Mechanics and Free Will	183
Chapter 16: The Observer Effect and Consciousness	185
Chapter 16.1: Definition of the Observer Effect	190
Chapter 16.2: The Role of the Observer Effect in Consciousness	192
Chapter 16.3: Experimental Evidence for the Observer Effect in Consciousness	195
Chapter 17: Quantum Mechanics and the Concept of Time	200
Chapter 17.1: The Definition of Time in Quantum Mechanics	205
Chapter 17.2: The Role of Time in Quantum Consciousness	207
Chapter 17.3: Criticisms of the Connection Between Quantum Mechanics and the Concept of Time	210
Chapter 18: Quantum Consciousness and the Afterlife	213
Chapter 18.1: The Connection Between Quantum Consciousness and the Afterlife	216
Chapter 18.2: The Implications of Quantum Consciousness for Life After Death	219
Chapter 18.3: Criticisms of the Connection Between	222

Quantum Consciousness and the Afterlife

Chapter 19: The Future of Quantum Consciousness Research — 224

Chapter 19.1: The Current State of Quantum Consciousness Research — 227

Chapter 19.2: The Challenges Facing Quantum Consciousness Research — 229

Chapter 19.3: The Promising Areas for Future Quantum Consciousness Research — 233

Chapter 20: Quantum Ethics — 235

Chapter 20.1: The Ethical Implications of Quantum Consciousness — 240

Chapter 20.2: The Role of Ethics in Quantum Consciousness Studies — 243

Chapter 20.3: The Need for Responsible Research in Quantum Consciousness — 246

Chapter 21: Conclusion — 249

Chapter 21.1: The Major Findings of Quantum Consciousness Studies — 251

Chapter 21.2: The Implications of Quantum Consciousness for Philosophy, Science, and Society — 254

Chapter 21.3: The Future Directions of Quantum Consciousness Research — 257

Chapter 21.4: The Ethical Implications of Quantum Consciousness — 260

For Further reading: — 263

Glossary of Terms for "Quantum Consciousness" — 265

Acknowledgement — 275

ABOUT THE AUTHOR — 277

Epilogue — 279

PREFACE

Have you ever wondered about the true nature of reality? About the way our thoughts, emotions, and experiences shape the world around us? If so, then "Reality Beyond the Veil: Revealing the True Nature of Reality with Quantum Conciseness" is the book for you.

In this book, we'll take a deep dive into the fascinating world of quantum physics and explore how our minds and the world around us are intimately connected. But don't worry if you're not a physics expert - this book is written in an easygoing, accessible style that makes even the most complex ideas simple to understand.

As someone who has long been fascinated by the mind-body connection, I wrote this book with the hope of helping readers unlock their full potential and create the life of their dreams. By understanding the mind-reality connection at a quantum level, we can become more mindful, intentional, and in control of our lives.

Throughout the book, you'll learn practical techniques for harnessing the power of your mind to create the reality you desire. You'll discover how our thoughts and emotions shape our experiences and how we can use this knowledge to manifest our goals.

I'm honored to share this journey with you and I hope that the insights and tools presented in this book will inspire and empower you to take control of your life and manifest the future you desire. So, let's get started on this fascinating exploration of the mind-reality connection at a quantum level!

INTRODUCTION

Welcome to "Reality Beyond the Veil: Revealing the True Nature of Reality with Quantum Concisenessl". This book is for anyone who is curious about the connection between our thoughts, emotions, and the world around us.

At first glance, the idea that our thoughts can shape our reality might seem like a far-fetched notion, but as we'll explore throughout this book, there is growing evidence from the field of quantum physics to support this concept. In fact, quantum physics suggests that the very act of observation can change the outcome of a physical experiment, highlighting the intimate connection between the observer and the observed.

In this book, we'll take a journey through the fascinating world of quantum physics and explore how it relates to our everyday lives. We'll examine how our thoughts and emotions can shape our reality, and learn practical techniques for harnessing this power to achieve our goals.

But this book is not just a scientific treatise. We'll also delve into the philosophical and spiritual implications of the mind-reality connection. We'll consider questions like: What is the nature of reality? What is the nature of consciousness? And, how can we use this knowledge to live a more fulfilling and harmonious existence?

My hope is that this book will inspire and empower you to take control of your life and manifest the future you desire. Whether you're a seasoned quantum enthusiast or a curious newcomer, I invite you to join me on this fascinating journey of exploration into the mind-reality connection at a quantum level.

Let's dive in!

Sai Venkatram

PROLOGUE

For centuries, philosophers, scientists, and spiritual leaders have explored the nature of reality and our place within it. But it wasn't until the advent of quantum physics that we began to truly grasp the incredible potential that lies within each of us.

In this book, "Reality Beyond the Veil: Revealing the True Nature of Reality with Quantum Conciseness", we'll dive deep into the mind-reality connection at a quantum level. But don't worry - you don't need to be a physics expert to understand the concepts we'll be exploring. Instead, we'll take an easygoing, down-to-earth approach that will help you grasp even the most complex ideas.

Along the way, we'll explore the fascinating world of quantum physics and how it relates to our everyday lives. We'll discuss the observer effect, entanglement, superposition, and much more. But this book isn't just a science lesson - it's a guide to living a more mindful, intentional life.

By understanding the connection between our thoughts, emotions, and reality, we can take control of our lives and manifest the future we desire. You'll learn practical techniques for harnessing the power of your mind to achieve your goals and create a more fulfilling existence.

So buckle up and get ready to explore the mind-reality connection like never before. Whether you're a quantum enthusiast or a curious newcomer,"Reality Beyond the Veil: Revealing the True Nature of Reality with Quantum Conciseness"will inspire and empower you to unlock your full potential and create the life of your dreams.

FOREWORD

As a physicist and student of the mind-body connection, I am excited to introduce "Reality Beyond the Veil: Revealing the True Nature of Reality with Quantum Conciseness" . This book is a wonderful guide for anyone who is curious about the connection between our thoughts, emotions, and the world around us.

In this easygoing guide,Sai Venkatram takes us on a journey through the fascinating world of quantum physics and how it relates to our everyday lives. You'll discover how our thoughts and emotions can shape our reality and learn practical techniques to harness this power to achieve our goals.

The concepts explored in this book are not just abstract ideas for scientific debate, they are concepts that can have a profound impact on our lives. By understanding the mind-reality consciousness at a quantum level, we can become more mindful and intentional in our lives, create a more harmonious and fulfilling existence, and manifest the future we desire.

I have no doubt that this book will inspire and empower readers to unlock their full potential and take control of their reality. So, whether you're a seasoned quantum enthusiast or a curious newcomer, I invite you to join me in exploring the incredible possibilities of the mind-reality connection.

A.Real Seeker!

CHAPTER 1: INTRODUCTION

Quantum mechanics and reality consciousness are two of the most fascinating and enigmatic fields of study known to humanity. Quantum mechanics deals with the strange and counterintuitive behavior of matter and energy at the subatomic level, while consciousness refers to the subjective experience of being aware and self-reflective.

Over the past few decades, a growing number of researchers and philosophers have explored the potential link between these two seemingly unrelated areas of inquiry. The idea that quantum mechanics may play a role in our understanding of consciousness has been both intriguing and controversial, with some dismissing it as pseudoscience and others embracing it as a new paradigm for understanding the nature of the mind.

"Reality Beyond the Veil: Revealing the True Nature of Reality with Quantum Conciseness" seeks to provide a comprehensive exploration of the concept of quantum consciousness, examining the scientific and philosophical arguments for and against this hypothesis. We will explore the history of these ideas, from early thinkers like Max Planck and Albert Einstein to contemporary scientists and thinkers like Roger Penrose, Stuart Hameroff, and David Chalmers.

We will delve into the mysterious nature of quantum mechanics and its implications for our understanding of the mind, exploring concepts such as entanglement, superposition, and coherence. We will also examine the challenges and criticisms faced by the quantum consciousness hypothesis, including the difficulty of reconciling quantum phenomena with the macroscopic world of human experience.

Throughout the book, we will also explore the practical applications of this hypothesis, from the development of new technologies to the potential impact on our understanding of mental illness and consciousness-altering practices such as meditation and psychedelics.

Ultimately, this book aims to provide readers with a nuanced and balanced understanding of the concept of quantum consciousness, allowing them to make informed decisions about its validity and potential implications. Whether you are a scientist, philosopher, or simply someone interested in the mysteries of the mind and the universe, this book is sure to provide a thought-provoking and illuminating exploration of this fascinating topic.

CHAPTER 1.1: WHAT IS QUANTUM CONSCIOUSNESS?

The concept of quantum consciousness proposes that quantum mechanics may play a role in the workings of the human mind. At its core, this hypothesis suggests that the strange and counterintuitive behavior of subatomic particles, such as superposition and entanglement, may also occur within the neural networks of the brain, giving rise to the subjective experience of consciousness.

While the concept of quantum consciousness remains controversial and highly debated, it is worth exploring some of the basic ideas and concepts that underpin this hypothesis.

One of the key ideas in quantum mechanics is the concept of superposition. At the subatomic level, particles such as electrons and photons can exist in multiple states simultaneously, known as superposition. This means that an electron can be in multiple places at once or have multiple properties, such as spin or energy, simultaneously.

Another important concept in quantum mechanics is entanglement. This occurs when two particles become intertwined, such that the state of one particle affects the state of the other, regardless of the distance between them. This strange and non-local connection between particles has been the subject of much study and speculation within the field of quantum mechanics.

Proponents of the concept of quantum consciousness suggest that these and other quantum phenomena may also occur within the neural networks of the brain, giving rise to the subjective experience of consciousness. According to this hypothesis, the brain may be able to exploit the strange and counterintuitive properties of quantum mechanics to process information in a more efficient and powerful way than classical computers.

However, the idea of quantum consciousness faces several challenges and criticisms. One of the main challenges is the difficulty of reconciling quantum phenomena with the macroscopic world of human experience. While quantum mechanics may hold true at the subatomic level, it is unclear how these strange and counterintuitive phenomena could give rise to the subjective experience of consciousness that we are familiar with.

Furthermore, critics of the quantum consciousness hypothesis argue that there is currently no empirical evidence to support the idea that quantum mechanics plays a role in consciousness. While some experiments have shown that certain biological systems, such as photosynthesis, may exhibit quantum behavior, it is unclear whether this can be extended to the workings of the human brain.

Despite these challenges and criticisms, the concept of quantum consciousness remains a fascinating and intriguing area of study. By exploring the intersection of quantum mechanics and consciousness, we may be able to gain new insights into the nature of the mind and the universe itself.

CHAPTER 1.2: THE HISTORY OF QUANTUM CONSCIOUSNESS

The concept of quantum consciousness has a rich and complex history, stretching back to the early days of quantum mechanics in the early 20th century. Many of the foundational ideas and concepts that underpin this hypothesis were first explored by pioneering scientists and thinkers of the time, including Max Planck and Albert Einstein.

In the early 1900s, Max Planck proposed that energy could only be emitted in discrete packets, or quanta, rather than in a continuous stream. This revolutionary idea formed the basis of quantum mechanics, which soon became a dominant force in the study of the subatomic world.

In the 1930s, Albert Einstein, Boris Podolsky, and Nathan Rosen proposed the concept of entanglement, in which two particles could become correlated in a way that defied classical physics. This strange and counterintuitive phenomenon would go on to become one of the defining features of quantum mechanics.

It was not until the latter half of the 20th century that scientists and philosophers began to explore the potential link between quantum mechanics and consciousness. In the 1960s and 1970s, thinkers such as John von Neumann and Eugene Wigner proposed that consciousness may be necessary to collapse the wave function, a fundamental concept in quantum mechanics that describes the probabilities of different states of a system.

In the 1980s, the physicist Roger Penrose and the anesthesiologist Stuart Hameroff proposed a specific theory of quantum consciousness, known as Orch-OR (orchestrated objective reduction). This theory suggests that microtubules, tiny structures within neurons, may be capable of exhibiting quantum behavior and could therefore be involved in the workings of the mind.

Since then, the concept of quantum consciousness has continued to attract the attention of researchers and thinkers from a wide range of fields, including physics, neuroscience, philosophy, and psychology. While the hypothesis remains highly controversial, it has also spurred a great deal of debate and discussion, leading to new insights and avenues of inquiry into the nature of the mind and the universe.

CHAPTER 1.3: WHY QUANTUM CONSCIOUSNESS MATTERS

The concept of quantum consciousness has the potential to revolutionize our understanding of the mind, consciousness, and the nature of reality itself. While the idea remains highly controversial and speculative, it is worth exploring some of the potential implications and applications of this hypothesis.

One of the most significant implications of quantum consciousness is that it could provide a new framework for understanding the subjective experience of consciousness. Traditional models of consciousness, such as the information-processing model, have struggled to fully account for the complex and multifaceted nature of consciousness. By exploring the potential link between quantum mechanics and consciousness, we may be able to gain new insights into this elusive and mysterious phenomenon.

Another potential application of quantum consciousness is in the field of artificial intelligence. While traditional computers rely on classical physics to process information, quantum computers are capable of exploiting the strange and counterintuitive properties of quantum mechanics to solve problems that would be impossible for classical computers. By exploring the potential link between quantum mechanics and the brain, we may be able to develop new models of artificial intelligence that more closely resemble the workings of the human mind.

In addition, the concept of quantum consciousness has the potential to shed new light on some of the most fundamental questions in physics and cosmology. For example, the strange and non-local connections between entangled particles could provide new insights into the nature of space-time and the fabric of the universe itself.

However, it is important to note that the concept of quantum consciousness remains highly speculative and controversial. While it has the potential to provide new insights and applications, it also faces many challenges and criticisms. As such, it is important to approach this hypothesis with a critical and open mind, while also recognizing its potential importance and significance.

CHAPTER 2: QUANTUM MECHANICS BASICS

To fully understand the concept of quantum consciousness, it is important to first have a basic understanding of quantum mechanics, the branch of physics that describes the behavior of matter and energy on a very small scale. In this chapter, we will explore some of the key concepts and principles of quantum mechanics that are relevant to the hypothesis of quantum consciousness.

Wave-Particle Duality

One of the key principles of quantum mechanics is wave-particle duality. This principle suggests that particles, such as electrons or photons, can exhibit both wave-like and particle-like behavior, depending on how they are observed or measured. For example, if an electron is observed as it passes through a slit, it behaves like a particle, producing a pattern on a detector screen. However, if the electron is not observed, it can exhibit wave-like behavior, producing an interference pattern on the detector screen. This strange and counterintuitive behavior is a fundamental feature of quantum mechanics.

The Uncertainty Principle

Another key principle of quantum mechanics is the uncertainty principle. This principle states that it is impossible to know both the position and momentum of a particle with absolute certainty. The more precisely one knows the position of a particle, the less precisely one can know its momentum, and vice versa. This principle is a consequence of wave-particle duality and is a fundamental limit on our ability to observe and measure the behavior of particles.

Superposition and Entanglement

Two other important concepts in quantum mechanics are superposition and entanglement. Superposition is the idea that a particle can exist in multiple states at the same time. For example, an electron can exist in a superposition of two energy states, with a certain probability of being in either state. Entanglement, on the other hand, is the idea that two particles can become correlated in a way that defies classical physics. When two particles are entangled, their states become intertwined, so that the state of one particle cannot be described without also describing the state of the other particle.

The Wave Function

The wave function is a central concept in quantum mechanics that describes the probabilities of different states of a system. The wave function is a complex mathematical function that describes the wave-like behavior of particles. When a particle is observed or measured, the wave function "collapses" to a single state, with a certain probability of being in that state. The collapse of the wave function is a key feature of quantum mechanics and is intimately tied to the concept of observation and measurement.

In conclusion, quantum mechanics is a complex and fascinating field of physics that has revolutionized our understanding of the universe. By exploring some of the key principles and concepts of quantum mechanics, we can gain a better understanding of the potential link between quantum mechanics and consciousness, and the implications and applications of this hypothesis.

CHAPTER 2.1: THE DOUBLE-SLIT EXPERIMENT

The double-slit experiment is one of the most famous and fundamental experiments in quantum mechanics. It was first performed by Thomas Young in the early 1800s and has since been repeated countless times, with increasingly sophisticated techniques and equipment.

The experiment involves shining a beam of light or a stream of particles, such as electrons or photons, through a barrier with two narrow slits. On the other side of the barrier, a detector screen records the pattern of the particles as they pass through the slits and interfere with each other.

The results of the experiment are striking and counterintuitive. When particles are fired through the slits one at a time, they produce a pattern on the detector screen that resembles the pattern produced by waves. This suggests that the particles are behaving like waves, interfering with each other and producing an interference pattern.

However, when particles are fired through the slits in a beam, they produce a pattern on the detector screen that resembles the pattern produced by particles. This suggests that the particles are behaving like particles, producing a distinct pattern on the detector screen.

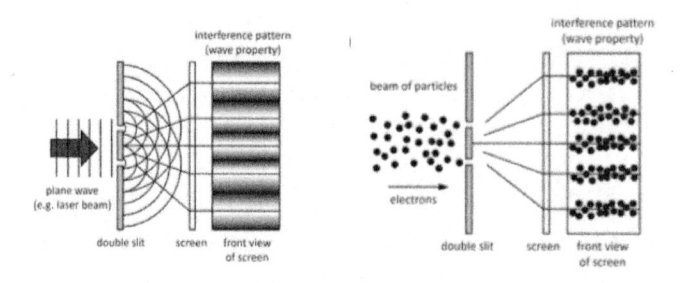

This strange and seemingly contradictory behavior can be explained by the principle of wave-particle duality. When particles are observed or measured, they behave like particles, producing a distinct pattern on the detector screen. However, when particles are not observed or measured, they behave like waves, interfering with each other and producing an interference pattern on the detector screen.

The double-slit experiment has profound implications for our understanding of the nature of reality and the role of observation and measurement in quantum mechanics. It suggests that the act of observation or measurement can influence the behavior of particles, collapsing the wave function and forcing particles to behave like particles. This raises the intriguing possibility that consciousness, as an act of observation and measurement, could play a role in the behavior of particles on a quantum level.

While the link between the double-slit experiment and consciousness remains highly speculative and controversial, it is worth exploring the potential implications and applications of this hypothesis. By understanding the fundamental principles of quantum mechanics, we can begin to unlock some of the mysteries of consciousness and the nature of reality itself.

One potential application of the hypothesis linking the double-slit experiment and consciousness is in the development of quantum computers. These computers use quantum mechanics principles to perform complex calculations much faster than classical computers.

It has been suggested that consciousness could play a role in the operation of quantum computers, potentially helping to control and manipulate the behavior of particles on a quantum level. This is a promising area of research, as quantum computers have the potential to revolutionize fields such as cryptography, materials science, and drug discovery.

Furthermore, the study of quantum consciousness could shed light on the nature of subjective experience and the relationship between the brain and consciousness. While the exact mechanisms underlying consciousness remain poorly understood, it is clear that the brain plays a crucial role.

By exploring the potential links between quantum mechanics and consciousness, we may be able to gain new insights into how the brain produces subjective experience and how consciousness arises from neural activity. This could have profound implications for our understanding of the human mind and our place in the universe.

In conclusion, the double-slit experiment is a fascinating and foundational experiment in quantum mechanics. While the link between the experiment and consciousness remains speculative, it is a hypothesis that is worth exploring. By studying the principles of quantum mechanics, we may be able to unlock some of the mysteries of consciousness and gain new insights into the nature of reality and the human mind.

CHAPTER 2.2: WAVE-PARTICLE DUALITY

Wave-particle duality is one of the fundamental principles of quantum mechanics. It describes how particles, such as electrons or photons, can exhibit both wave-like and particle-like behavior depending on how they are observed or measured.

The concept of wave-particle duality was first introduced by Louis de Broglie in 1924. He proposed that particles, such as electrons, could also have wave-like properties, such as wavelength and frequency. This was confirmed in the double-slit experiment, where particles were observed to produce an interference pattern on a detector screen, suggesting that they were behaving like waves.

However, when particles are observed or measured, they behave like particles, producing a distinct pattern on the detector screen. This is known as wave function collapse, where the probability distribution of a particle collapses into a single outcome upon observation or measurement.

The phenomenon of wave-particle duality has profound implications for our understanding of the nature of reality and the role of observation and measurement in quantum mechanics. It suggests that the act of observation or measurement can influence the behavior of particles, collapsing the wave function and forcing particles to behave like particles.

This raises the intriguing possibility that consciousness, as an act of observation and measurement, could play a role in the behavior of particles on a quantum level. Some scientists and philosophers have suggested that consciousness may be a fundamental aspect of the universe, influencing the behavior of particles and contributing to the nature of reality itself.

While the idea of consciousness influencing quantum mechanics remains highly speculative and controversial, the concept of wave-particle duality remains a foundational principle in quantum mechanics. It has important applications in fields such as quantum computing, where particles are manipulated to perform complex calculations, and in the study of the behavior of atoms and molecules.

In conclusion, wave-particle duality is a fundamental principle of quantum mechanics that describes how particles can exhibit both wave-like and particle-like behavior depending on how they are observed or measured. It has profound implications for our understanding of the nature of reality and the potential role of consciousness in quantum mechanics. Further research in this area may lead to new insights into the mysteries of the universe and the human mind.

observed
"here"

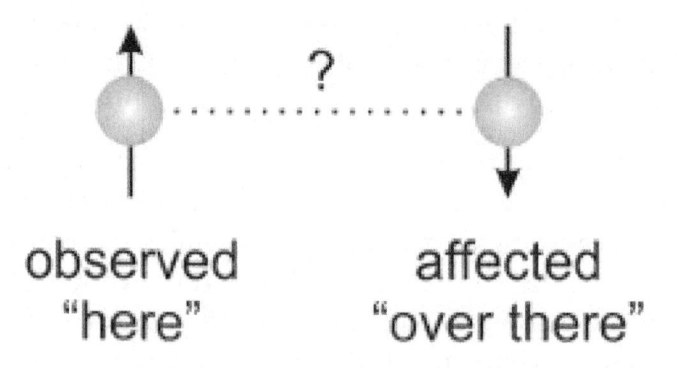

affected
"over there"

CHAPTER 2.3: QUANTUM ENTANGLEMENT

Quantum entanglement is a phenomenon in quantum mechanics where particles become connected in such a way that the state of one particle is dependent on the state of the other, regardless of the distance between them. This means that if the state of one particle is changed, the state of the other particle will also change instantaneously, even if they are separated by vast distances.

This seemingly paradoxical phenomenon was first described by Albert Einstein, Boris Podolsky, and Nathan Rosen in 1935. They proposed the EPR paradox, which suggested that quantum mechanics was incomplete and that there must be some hidden variables that governed the behavior of particles, making entanglement impossible.

However, in 1964, physicist John Bell proposed a way to test whether entanglement was real or simply a result of hidden variables. His famous Bell's inequality theorem showed that if quantum mechanics was correct, then certain measurements made on entangled particles would violate a mathematical inequality. These measurements have since been performed, and the results have consistently shown that entanglement is indeed a real phenomenon.

The concept of entanglement has important applications in fields such as quantum cryptography, where entangled particles are used to transmit secure messages, and quantum teleportation, where the state of a particle is transferred from one location to another instantaneously.

Furthermore, entanglement has also been proposed as a potential mechanism for communication between conscious entities, such as humans or animals. While the idea of quantum communication between conscious entities remains highly speculative, it has led to new avenues of research in the study of consciousness and the nature of reality.

In conclusion, quantum entanglement is a real phenomenon in quantum mechanics where particles become connected in such a way that their states are dependent on each other, regardless of the distance between them. This has important applications in fields such as quantum cryptography and quantum teleportation, and has also led to new avenues of research in the study of consciousness and the nature of reality.

CHAPTER 3: THE BRAIN AND CONSCIOUSNESS

The human brain is one of the most complex structures in the known universe, and it is the organ responsible for our consciousness. While there is still much to be discovered about the brain and how it produces consciousness, there have been significant advances in our understanding of the neural mechanisms that underlie conscious experience.

Neurons are the building blocks of the brain, and they communicate with each other through electrical and chemical signals. These signals create patterns of activity that can be measured using techniques such as electroencephalography (EEG) and functional magnetic resonance imaging (fMRI).

One of the most widely studied aspects of the neural correlates of consciousness is the concept of neural synchrony. Neural synchrony refers to the coordinated firing of groups of neurons, which has been linked to conscious experience. For example, when individuals are shown a visual stimulus, there is an increase in synchrony in certain brain regions, suggesting that these regions are involved in processing the visual information and generating conscious experience.

Another important aspect of the brain and consciousness is the concept of neural plasticity. Neural plasticity refers to the brain's ability to change and adapt in response to experience. This is important for learning and memory, and it is thought to play a role in the formation of conscious experience. For example, repeated exposure to a stimulus can lead to changes in the brain that allow for faster and more efficient processing of that stimulus, which can influence conscious experience.

While our understanding of the neural mechanisms of consciousness has advanced significantly in recent years, there are still many unanswered questions. One of the most intriguing questions is whether quantum mechanics plays a role in the brain and consciousness.

There is growing interest in the idea of quantum consciousness, which proposes that consciousness arises from quantum processes in the brain. This idea is based on the notion that the brain's neural processes involve the exchange of small packets of energy, or quanta, which could exhibit quantum mechanical behavior.

While the idea of quantum consciousness is still highly speculative and controversial, it has led to new avenues of research in the study of consciousness and the brain. By understanding the neural mechanisms of consciousness, as well as the potential role of quantum mechanics, we may be able to unlock some of the mysteries of the brain and consciousness.

One of the key challenges in understanding the relationship between quantum mechanics and consciousness is that the brain is a warm, wet, and noisy environment, which is very different from the cold, isolated, and stable conditions typically required for quantum mechanical effects to be observed. As a result, it is unclear whether the delicate and fragile nature of quantum states can be maintained in the brain long enough to contribute to consciousness.

Despite these challenges, there have been several intriguing findings that suggest a potential link between quantum mechanics and consciousness. For example, some studies have suggested that certain proteins in the brain may exhibit quantum mechanical behavior, which could have implications for the functioning of neurons and the formation of conscious experience.

Other researchers have proposed that quantum mechanics may play a role in the phenomenon of neural synchrony, which we discussed earlier. They suggest that quantum entanglement could be responsible for the coordinated firing of groups of neurons, which is associated with conscious experience.

While these ideas are still speculative, they highlight the potential importance of quantum mechanics in understanding the brain and consciousness. Furthermore, they provide new avenues for research and experimentation that could help to shed light on the mysteries of consciousness.

In the next chapter, we will explore some of the philosophical and metaphysical implications of quantum consciousness, including its potential implications for the nature of reality itself.

CHAPTER 3.1: THE NEUROBIOLOGICAL BASIS OF CONSCIOUSNESS

The quest to understand consciousness has been a central focus of neuroscience for many years. Researchers have made significant progress in identifying the neural correlates of consciousness, which are the patterns of neural activity that are associated with subjective experiences of perception, thought, and emotion.

One of the key insights in this field has been the recognition that consciousness arises from the integrated activity of large-scale neural networks. These networks are thought to involve multiple brain regions, which work together to create a coherent and unified experience of the world.

Neuroimaging studies have provided strong evidence for this view, showing that conscious experiences are associated with the coordinated activity of widespread brain regions, including the prefrontal cortex, parietal cortex, and temporal lobes. These regions are known to be involved in a range of cognitive processes, including attention, perception, memory, and decision-making.

Recent research has also suggested that the thalamus, a small but crucial structure deep within the brain, may play a key role in regulating the flow of information between different brain regions and thus contribute to the formation of conscious experience.

While these findings have shed light on the neural basis of consciousness, they do not provide a complete understanding of how subjective experiences arise from the activity of neurons. This is where the potential role of quantum mechanics comes into play.

In the next section, we will explore how quantum mechanics could contribute to our understanding of consciousness by exploring the possibility of quantum coherence in the brain.

CHAPTER 3.2: THE HARD PROBLEM OF CONSCIOUSNESS

While progress has been made in identifying the neural correlates of consciousness, there remains a fundamental mystery at the heart of our understanding of subjective experience - the so-called "hard problem" of consciousness.

The hard problem of consciousness refers to the challenge of explaining how the activity of neurons gives rise to the subjective experience of consciousness. Even if we can identify the specific neural correlates of consciousness, it is not clear how these patterns of activity could give rise to subjective experiences such as the taste of chocolate, the sound of music, or the feeling of love.

This is a problem that has puzzled philosophers, neuroscientists, and cognitive scientists for many years. Some have argued that it is simply an insurmountable challenge - that there is no way to bridge the "explanatory gap" between neural activity and subjective experience.

Others have proposed that the solution may lie in the nature of consciousness itself, rather than in the activity of neurons. For example, philosopher David Chalmers has argued that consciousness may be a fundamental property of the universe, in the same way that space and time are. This would mean that consciousness is not simply an emergent property of complex systems like the brain, but rather an irreducible aspect of reality itself.

The hard problem of consciousness remains one of the most intriguing and challenging questions in science, and it is not clear whether we will ever be able to fully solve it. However, by exploring the potential role of quantum mechanics in consciousness, we may be able to shed new light on this mystery and bring us closer to a more complete understanding of the nature of subjective experience.

One of the most promising avenues for exploring the hard problem of consciousness is through the lens of quantum mechanics. Some researchers have proposed that quantum mechanics may be able to provide a framework for understanding how subjective experience arises from neural activity.

One theory, known as Orchestrated Objective Reduction (Orch-OR), was proposed by neuroscientist Stuart Hameroff and physicist Roger Penrose. Orch-OR suggests that the microtubules inside neurons may be able to support quantum states, and that these quantum states could contribute to the emergence of consciousness.

According to Orch-OR, the collapse of quantum states in microtubules could trigger a process known as objective reduction, which would result in a conscious experience. This theory has been met with both skepticism and interest, and has spurred new research into the potential role of quantum mechanics in consciousness.

Other researchers have proposed that the entanglement of quantum states across different parts of the brain could be responsible for the integration of information required for conscious experience. By understanding the nature of this entanglement, we may be able to gain new insights into the neural mechanisms underlying consciousness.

While the role of quantum mechanics in consciousness remains highly speculative and controversial, it is clear that this area of research is opening up new avenues for exploring the nature of subjective experience. By bringing together insights from neuroscience, physics, and philosophy, we may be able to shed new light on one of the greatest mysteries of the human experience - the nature of consciousness.

CHAPTER 3.3: THE INTEGRATED INFORMATION THEORY OF CONSCIOUSNESS

The Integrated Information Theory (IIT) of consciousness is a leading framework for understanding the neural basis of subjective experience. Proposed by neuroscientist Giulio Tononi, IIT posits that consciousness arises from the integrated information generated by the brain.

According to IIT, consciousness is not tied to specific brain regions or processes, but rather emerges from the complex interactions and information flow between neurons. This integrated information is characterized by a high degree of irreducibility and specificity - meaning that it cannot be reduced to the properties of individual neurons or systems, and that it is unique to a particular conscious experience.

IIT also provides a mathematical framework for quantifying the degree of integrated information generated by a system, known as phi. Higher levels of phi are thought to correspond to a greater degree of consciousness and subjective experience.

While IIT does not explicitly incorporate quantum mechanics, some researchers have proposed that quantum effects could contribute to the generation of integrated information. For example, the entanglement of quantum states across different parts of the brain could facilitate the integration of information required for conscious experience.

According to the IIT, consciousness is not something that is simply present or absent in a given system, but rather it exists on a spectrum. Consciousness is measured in terms of integrated information, or the amount of information that is present in a system that cannot be divided into independent parts. In other words, consciousness emerges when information is integrated in a way that creates a whole that is greater than the sum of its parts.

To understand how the IIT works, it is helpful to consider the example of a computer. A computer is capable of processing vast amounts of information, but it is not conscious because the information is processed in a way that is modular and independent. The processing of information in a computer is divided into discrete components, each of which can be replaced or removed without affecting the functioning of the system as a whole.

On the other hand, the brain is capable of integrating information in a way that creates a unified experience of consciousness. This is because the information in the brain is processed in a way that is highly interconnected and cannot be divided into independent parts. The neurons in the brain are constantly communicating with one another, creating a complex network of information that is integrated in a way that creates a unified experience of consciousness.

The IIT also proposes that consciousness is a fundamental aspect of the universe, and that it exists in all systems that are capable of integrating information in a way that creates a whole that is greater than the sum of its parts. This means that consciousness is not unique to humans or other animals, but rather it exists in all systems that are capable of processing and integrating information.

One of the key implications of the IIT is that consciousness cannot be reduced to any particular neural activity or brain region. Instead, consciousness emerges from the integrated information that is present in the brain as a whole. This means that any attempt to identify a specific location in the brain that is responsible for consciousness is misguided.

The IIT has been the subject of significant debate and criticism since its inception, with some researchers arguing that it is too vague and difficult to test empirically. However, it has also received significant support from other researchers, who believe that it provides a promising framework for understanding the complex relationship between the brain and consciousness.

Overall, the IIT represents an important step forward in our understanding of consciousness and the brain. While much more research is needed to fully understand how consciousness arises in the brain, the IIT provides a useful framework for exploring this fascinating and elusive phenomenon.

CHAPTER 4: QUANTUM INFORMATION THEORY

Quantum Information Theory is a branch of physics that studies how information can be encoded, transmitted, and processed using quantum mechanical systems. This field has gained significant attention in recent years due to its potential applications in various fields, including cryptography, computation, and communication.

In this chapter, we will explore the basics of quantum information theory and its potential implications for understanding the relationship between quantum mechanics and consciousness.

The Basics of Quantum Information Theory

Quantum information theory is based on the principles of quantum mechanics, which describes the behavior of matter and energy at the atomic and subatomic levels. In classical information theory, information is represented as bits, which can have a value of either 0 or 1. In quantum information theory, information is represented as quantum bits, or qubits, which can have a value of 0, 1, or a superposition of both.

The most famous example of a qubit is the spin of an electron. An electron can have a spin that is either "up" or "down," but it can also exist in a superposition of both states. This means that a qubit can exist in a state of "0," "1," or a combination of both states simultaneously.

The ability of qubits to exist in a superposition of states is one of the key features of quantum information theory. This property allows quantum systems to process information in ways that are impossible for classical systems. For example, a quantum computer could potentially solve certain problems much faster than a classical computer by exploiting the power of superposition and entanglement.

Entanglement is another key feature of quantum information theory. When two qubits are entangled, they become correlated in a way that is impossible for classical systems. This means that when the state of one qubit is measured, the state of the other qubit is instantly determined, regardless of the distance between them.

Quantum Information Theory and Consciousness

The potential implications of quantum information theory for understanding the relationship between quantum mechanics and consciousness have been the subject of significant debate and speculation. One theory, known as the Orch OR theory, proposes that consciousness arises from quantum processes that occur within microtubules in the brain.

According to this theory, the microtubules in neurons act as quantum computers, processing and integrating information in ways that are impossible for classical systems. The quantum processes in these microtubules are thought to give rise to consciousness by creating coherent states of consciousness that are distributed throughout the brain.

While the Orch OR theory is controversial and has been criticized by many researchers, it represents an interesting application of quantum information theory to the study of consciousness. Other researchers have explored the potential role of quantum processes in the brain, such as the possibility that entanglement may play a role in neural communication.

Conclusion

Quantum information theory represents an exciting and rapidly evolving field of research that has the potential to revolutionize our understanding of information processing and communication. While the potential implications of this theory for understanding the relationship between quantum mechanics and consciousness are still largely speculative, the continued exploration of this field may eventually lead to new insights into one of the most mysterious phenomena in the universe.

CHAPTER 4.1: QUANTUM BITS (QUBITS)

In quantum information theory, information is represented as quantum bits, or qubits. Unlike classical bits, which can only have a value of either 0 or 1, qubits can exist in a superposition of states, which means they can have a value of 0, 1, or a combination of both simultaneously.

This ability to exist in a superposition of states is one of the key features of qubits, and it enables quantum systems to process information in ways that are impossible for classical systems. For example, a quantum computer can potentially solve certain problems much faster than a classical computer by exploiting the power of superposition and entanglement.

Types of Qubits

There are several different types of qubits, including:

Superconducting qubits

These are qubits that are fabricated from superconducting materials and are used in many quantum computing systems. Superconducting qubits are typically implemented using small loops of wire called Josephson junctions.

Ion trap qubits

These are qubits that are implemented using trapped ions. The qubit is represented by the spin state of the ion, which can be manipulated using laser beams.

Quantum dot qubits

These are qubits that are implemented using semiconductor materials. The qubit is represented by the spin state of an electron confined to a quantum dot.

Photonic qubits

These are qubits that are implemented using photons, which are particles of light. Photonic qubits can be transmitted over long distances using optical fibers, which makes them useful for quantum communication.

Encoding Information in Qubits

Information can be encoded in qubits using a variety of techniques. One common technique is to use the polarization state of photons to represent information. In this scheme, a qubit can be in a state of either horizontal polarization or vertical polarization, which correspond to the values 0 and 1, respectively.

Another common technique is to use the spin state of an electron or ion to represent information. In this scheme, a qubit can be in a state of either "up" or "down," which correspond to the values 0 and 1, respectively.

Entanglement and Qubits

One of the most fascinating features of qubits is entanglement. When two qubits are entangled, they become correlated in a way that is impossible for classical systems. This means that when the state of one qubit is measured, the state of the other qubit is instantly determined, regardless of the distance between them.

Entanglement is a powerful resource for quantum information processing, and it has important implications for understanding the relationship between quantum mechanics and consciousness. Some researchers have proposed that entanglement may play a role in neural communication and may be involved in the emergence of consciousness.

Conclusion

Quantum bits, or qubits, are a fundamental concept in quantum information theory. They enable quantum systems to process information in ways that are impossible for classical systems, and they have important implications for quantum computing and quantum communication. Entanglement, which is a key feature of qubits, is a powerful resource for quantum information processing and may also have implications for understanding the relationship between quantum mechanics and consciousness.

CHAPTER 4.2: QUANTUM GATES

In quantum computing, quantum gates are the equivalent of logic gates in classical computing. They are the basic building blocks of quantum circuits and are used to manipulate the state of qubits.

Quantum gates can be thought of as mathematical operations that transform the state of one or more qubits into another state. These operations can be represented using matrices, and the matrix representation of a quantum gate is known as its unitary matrix.

Types of Quantum Gates
There are several types of quantum gates, including:

Pauli gates
> These are the most basic quantum gates and are used to flip the state of a qubit. There are three types of Pauli gates: X, Y, and Z.

Hadamard gate
> This gate is used to put a qubit into a superposition of states.

CNOT gate
> This gate is used to entangle two qubits. It applies a NOT operation to one qubit (the target qubit) if and only if another qubit (the control qubit) is in a particular state.

Phase gate

This gate is used to introduce a phase shift into the state of a qubit.

T gate
This gate is used to introduce a quarter-phase shift into the state of a qubit.

SWAP gate
This gate is used to exchange the state of two qubits.

Applications of Quantum Gates

Quantum gates are essential for quantum computation, as they enable the manipulation of qubits in order to perform calculations. By applying a series of quantum gates to a set of qubits, it is possible to create complex quantum circuits that can perform specific computational tasks.

In addition to quantum computation, quantum gates also have applications in quantum communication and quantum cryptography. For example, quantum gates can be used to create entangled states of photons, which can then be used to transmit information securely over long distances.

Quantum Gates and Consciousness

The study of quantum consciousness proposes that quantum processes within the brain may be responsible for the emergence of consciousness. While there is still much debate and controversy around this idea, some researchers have suggested that quantum gates and entanglement may play a role in neural communication and information processing in the brain.

Conclusion

Quantum gates are the basic building blocks of quantum circuits and are used to manipulate the state of qubits. They enable quantum computation, communication, and cryptography, and they have important implications for understanding the relationship between quantum mechanics and consciousness. The study of quantum consciousness proposes that quantum gates and entanglement may play a role in neural communication and the emergence of consciousness, although this idea remains controversial and is still the subject of ongoing research.

CHAPTER 4.3: QUANTUM ALGORITHMS

Quantum algorithms are computational procedures designed to run on quantum computers, leveraging the unique properties of qubits to perform calculations that would be infeasible or impossible on classical computers. In this chapter, we will discuss some of the most famous quantum algorithms and their potential applications in quantum consciousness research.

Grover's Algorithm

Grover's algorithm is a quantum search algorithm that can be used to search through an unsorted database of N items in O(sqrt(N)) time, a significant speedup over classical algorithms that require O(N) time. Grover's algorithm achieves this speedup by using quantum superposition and interference to amplify the probability of finding the desired item.

In the context of quantum consciousness, Grover's algorithm could potentially be used to search through large datasets of neural activity and identify patterns or correlations that are difficult to discern using classical algorithms.

Shor's Algorithm

Shor's algorithm is a quantum algorithm for factoring large integers into their prime factors. Shor's algorithm is exponentially faster than the best-known classical algorithms for factoring, which rely on the difficulty of the integer factorization problem for cryptography.

In the context of quantum consciousness, Shor's algorithm could be used to factor large numbers that arise in the study of quantum field theory or other models of quantum mechanics that have been proposed as potential explanations for the relationship between quantum mechanics and consciousness.

Deutsch-Jozsa Algorithm

The Deutsch-Jozsa algorithm is a quantum algorithm for determining whether a Boolean function is constant or balanced. The algorithm achieves a quadratic speedup over classical algorithms for this problem, which would require a linear number of evaluations to determine the nature of the function.

In the context of quantum consciousness, the Deutsch-Jozsa algorithm could potentially be used to analyze the nature of neural firing patterns and determine whether they exhibit any underlying structure or regularity that would be difficult to detect using classical algorithms.

Quantum Walks

Quantum walks are a class of quantum algorithms that simulate random walks on graphs or other structures. Quantum walks have been used to solve a variety of optimization and search problems, and they have also been proposed as a model for neural information processing in the brain.

In the context of quantum consciousness, quantum walks could be used to study the dynamics of information flow within neural networks and explore the relationship between quantum mechanics and the emergence of consciousness.

Conclusion

Quantum algorithms are an essential component of quantum information theory and have the potential to revolutionize computing, communication, and cryptography. In the context of quantum consciousness, quantum algorithms could be used to analyze large datasets of neural activity, factor large numbers that arise in quantum models of consciousness, and explore the dynamics of information flow within neural networks. While much work remains to be done in this field, quantum algorithms hold great promise for shedding light on the relationship between quantum mechanics and consciousness.

CHAPTER 5: QUANTUM COMPUTERS AND CONSCIOUSNESS

In this chapter, we will explore the potential connections between quantum computers and consciousness. As we have discussed earlier, quantum computers have the potential to revolutionize computing and information processing, and they may also provide insights into the nature of consciousness.

Quantum Computers and Brain Simulations

One of the most promising applications of quantum computers in the study of consciousness is the simulation of the brain. The human brain is one of the most complex and least understood systems in the universe, with billions of neurons interacting in highly nonlinear ways. Classical computers struggle to simulate even small-scale models of the brain, and it is unclear whether they will ever be able to simulate the full complexity of the brain.

Quantum computers, on the other hand, may be well-suited to simulating the brain due to their ability to process vast amounts of data in parallel and their potential for quantum entanglement. Some researchers have proposed using quantum computers to simulate neural activity in the brain and explore the relationship between quantum mechanics and consciousness.

Quantum Computers and the Hard Problem of Consciousness

The hard problem of consciousness refers to the

philosophical problem of explaining subjective experience in terms of physical processes. While classical computers can simulate the behavior of physical systems, they struggle to account for the subjective experience of consciousness. Quantum computers may offer a potential solution to this problem by providing a more comprehensive model of physical reality.

Some researchers have proposed that the phenomenon of quantum entanglement, in which two particles become correlated in such a way that their properties are no longer independent, may provide a clue to the nature of subjective experience. If consciousness arises from the underlying quantum mechanics of the brain, then the entanglement of particles within the brain may be crucial to understanding consciousness.

Quantum Computers and the Future of Consciousness Research

While much work remains to be done in the field of quantum consciousness, quantum computers hold great promise for shedding light on the nature of consciousness. By simulating neural activity in the brain, exploring the relationship between quantum mechanics and consciousness, and providing a more comprehensive model of physical reality, quantum computers may help us unlock the secrets of consciousness and pave the way for new treatments for disorders of consciousness.

Conclusion

Quantum computers represent a major breakthrough in computing and information processing, and they may also provide insights into the nature of consciousness. By simulating neural activity in the brain, exploring the relationship between quantum mechanics and consciousness, and providing a more comprehensive model of physical reality, quantum computers may help us solve the hard problem of consciousness and revolutionize our understanding of the mind. As we continue to develop more powerful and sophisticated quantum computers, we may be on the brink of a new era in consciousness research.

CHAPTER 5.1: THE POTENTIAL OF QUANTUM COMPUTING FOR CONSCIOUSNESS STUDIES

In this section, we will explore in more detail the potential of quantum computing for studying consciousness. While much work remains to be done in this field, quantum computers offer several advantages over classical computers when it comes to simulating and understanding the brain and consciousness.

Parallel Processing and Neural Networks

One of the key advantages of quantum computers is their ability to perform many calculations simultaneously through the use of superposition and entanglement. This makes them well-suited to simulating neural networks in the brain, which rely on the parallel processing of information by many neurons.

Neural networks are highly complex and nonlinear systems, making them difficult to simulate using classical computers. By contrast, quantum computers may be able to simulate the behavior of neurons and neural networks more accurately and efficiently.

Quantum Entanglement and Consciousness

Quantum entanglement is a phenomenon in which two particles become correlated in such a way that their properties are no longer independent. Some researchers have proposed that this phenomenon may be relevant to the study of consciousness.

In particular, it has been suggested that the entanglement of particles within the brain may be crucial to understanding subjective experience. If consciousness arises from the underlying quantum mechanics of the brain, then the entanglement of particles within the brain may be responsible for generating the integrated and coherent experience of consciousness.

Simulating Brain Activity with Quantum Computers

The human brain is one of the most complex systems in the universe, with billions of neurons interacting in highly nonlinear ways. Simulating the behavior of the brain on a classical computer is a daunting task, requiring massive amounts of computational power and memory.

Quantum computers may be well-suited to simulating brain activity due to their ability to perform many calculations in parallel and their potential for quantum entanglement. By simulating the behavior of neural networks on a quantum computer, researchers may be able to gain new insights into the functioning of the brain and the nature of consciousness.

Conclusion

While much work remains to be done in the field of quantum consciousness, quantum computers hold great promise for shedding light on the nature of consciousness. By simulating neural activity in the brain, exploring the relationship between quantum mechanics and consciousness, and providing a more comprehensive model of physical reality, quantum computers may help us unlock the secrets of consciousness and pave the way for new treatments for disorders of consciousness. As the field of quantum computing continues to evolve and mature, we may be on the brink of a new era in consciousness research.

CHAPTER 5.2: THE CHALLENGES OF BUILDING A QUANTUM COMPUTER FOR CONSCIOUSNESS STUDIES

While quantum computers offer great potential for studying consciousness, building a working quantum computer is a highly challenging task. In this section, we will explore some of the major challenges facing researchers who seek to build a quantum computer for consciousness studies.

Quantum Decoherence

One of the biggest challenges facing quantum computing is quantum decoherence. This occurs when a quantum system interacts with its environment, causing it to lose its coherence and become a classical system.

Quantum computers rely on the precise manipulation of quantum states to perform calculations, and any interference from the environment can disrupt these delicate states. This poses a significant challenge for building a quantum computer that can accurately simulate the behavior of the brain.

Error Correction

Another challenge facing quantum computing is the issue of error correction. Because quantum systems are highly sensitive to their environment, even small errors can quickly accumulate and make computations useless.

To address this issue, researchers are developing new error correction techniques that can detect and correct errors in quantum computations. However, these techniques are still in their early stages, and it remains to be seen whether they will be effective enough to allow for large-scale quantum computing.

Scalability

Finally, one of the biggest challenges facing quantum computing is scalability. While quantum computers have already demonstrated impressive feats of computation, they are still far from being able to simulate the complexity of the human brain.

To build a quantum computer capable of simulating neural networks, researchers will need to develop new hardware and software architectures that can scale up to accommodate billions of qubits. This will require significant advances in materials science, engineering, and computer science.

Conclusion

Building a quantum computer for consciousness studies is an incredibly ambitious goal that will require significant advances in multiple fields of research. While quantum computers offer great promise for understanding the nature of consciousness and simulating the behavior of the brain, researchers will need to overcome significant challenges related to quantum decoherence, error correction, and scalability.

Despite these challenges, the potential benefits of quantum computing for consciousness studies make the effort worth pursuing. With continued investment and innovation, it may be possible to build a quantum computer capable of simulating the behavior of the brain and shedding new light on the mysteries of consciousness.

CHAPTER 5.3: THE FUTURE OF QUANTUM COMPUTING AND CONSCIOUSNESS STUDIES

Quantum computing has the potential to revolutionize our understanding of consciousness and the brain. While researchers face significant challenges in building a quantum computer capable of simulating the behavior of the brain, the potential benefits make the effort worthwhile.

In this section, we will explore some of the exciting possibilities for the future of quantum computing and consciousness studies.

Simulating the Brain

One of the most promising applications of quantum computing for consciousness studies is the ability to simulate the behavior of the brain. By creating a quantum computer capable of simulating the activity of billions of neurons, researchers could gain new insights into the nature of consciousness and the brain.

This could lead to new treatments for neurological disorders, as well as a deeper understanding of the fundamental nature of human cognition.

Quantum Artificial Intelligence

Another exciting possibility for the future of quantum

computing and consciousness studies is the development of quantum artificial intelligence. By combining the power of quantum computing with advanced machine learning algorithms, researchers could create new forms of intelligent systems that are capable of self-learning and adapting to new situations.

This could lead to new breakthroughs in the field of robotics, as well as new approaches to understanding the nature of human intelligence and consciousness.

Quantum Cryptography

Finally, quantum computing could also have significant implications for the field of cryptography. Quantum cryptography uses the laws of quantum mechanics to create unbreakable codes that cannot be cracked by conventional computers.

This could have significant implications for protecting sensitive information related to consciousness studies, as well as other fields of research.

Conclusion

The future of quantum computing and consciousness studies is full of exciting possibilities. While researchers still face significant challenges in building a quantum computer capable of simulating the behavior of the brain, the potential benefits make the effort worthwhile.

From simulating the brain and developing quantum artificial intelligence to enhancing cybersecurity, quantum computing could transform our understanding of consciousness and the world around us. With continued investment and innovation, the future of quantum computing and consciousness studies is sure to be full of exciting new breakthroughs and discoveries.

CHAPTER 6: THE QUANTUM ZENO EFFECT

The Quantum Zeno effect is a phenomenon in quantum mechanics that has been proposed as a potential explanation for the relationship between consciousness and the measurement problem in quantum mechanics. In this chapter, we will explore the Quantum Zeno effect and its implications for consciousness studies.

What is the Quantum Zeno Effect?

The Quantum Zeno effect refers to the observation that a quantum system that is continuously observed or measured is prevented from undergoing certain changes. This effect is named after the Greek philosopher Zeno, who was known for his paradoxes involving motion.

In quantum mechanics, the Quantum Zeno effect occurs when a system is continuously observed or measured, preventing it from undergoing a quantum transition. Essentially, the act of observing or measuring the system keeps it in its current state and prevents it from evolving into another state.

Implications for Consciousness Studies

The Quantum Zeno effect has been proposed as a potential explanation for the role of consciousness in the measurement problem in quantum mechanics. According to this hypothesis, the act of conscious observation or measurement can cause the Quantum Zeno effect, preventing the collapse of the wave function and maintaining the superposition of states.

This has led some researchers to suggest that consciousness may be a fundamental property of the universe, and that the act of conscious observation or measurement may be necessary for the collapse of the wave function.

Critics of this hypothesis argue that it is not necessary to invoke consciousness to explain the Quantum Zeno effect, and that other factors such as environmental decoherence may play a role.

Experimental Evidence

While the role of consciousness in the Quantum Zeno effect remains controversial, there is experimental evidence that supports the effect itself. In one experiment, researchers used laser pulses to repeatedly measure the state of an ion in a trap, preventing it from undergoing a quantum transition.

Other experiments have also demonstrated the Quantum Zeno effect in various quantum systems, providing further evidence for the phenomenon.

Conclusion

The Quantum Zeno effect is a fascinating phenomenon in quantum mechanics that has potential implications for consciousness studies. While the role of consciousness in the effect remains controversial, there is experimental evidence that supports the effect itself.

As research in quantum mechanics and consciousness studies continues to progress, the Quantum Zeno effect will likely remain an area of ongoing interest and exploration. Its potential implications for our understanding of the relationship between consciousness and the fundamental nature of the universe make it an intriguing area for further investigation.

6.1: DEFINITION OF THE QUANTUM ZENO EFFECT

The Quantum Zeno effect is a phenomenon in quantum mechanics that occurs when a quantum system is continuously observed or measured, preventing it from undergoing certain changes. It is named after the Greek philosopher Zeno, who was known for his paradoxes involving motion.

In quantum mechanics, the Quantum Zeno effect occurs when a system is observed or measured frequently enough to prevent it from undergoing a quantum transition. Essentially, the act of observing or measuring the system keeps it in its current state and prevents it from evolving into another state.

This effect has been observed in various quantum systems, including atoms, ions, and photons, and has been proposed as a potential explanation for the role of consciousness in the measurement problem in quantum mechanics.

While the exact mechanism behind the Quantum Zeno effect remains a subject of debate and research, its potential implications for our understanding of the fundamental nature of the universe and the role of consciousness make it an area of ongoing interest and exploration in both quantum mechanics and consciousness studies.

The Quantum Zeno effect has been proposed as a potential explanation for the role of consciousness in the measurement problem in quantum mechanics. The measurement problem refers to the mysterious phenomenon in quantum mechanics where the act of measurement or observation seems to collapse the wave function, causing a quantum system to collapse into a definite state.

Some researchers have proposed that consciousness, as an active observer, could play a role in the Quantum Zeno effect and the measurement problem. They suggest that the constant monitoring and observation of quantum systems by conscious beings could be responsible for the observed effects.

However, this idea remains controversial, and many scientists and philosophers argue that consciousness alone cannot account for the quantum Zeno effect or the measurement problem. They suggest that other physical mechanisms, such as decoherence, may be responsible for these effects.

Despite the ongoing debate, the Quantum Zeno effect remains an important and fascinating area of research in both quantum mechanics and consciousness studies. Its potential implications for our understanding of the fundamental nature of reality and the role of consciousness in the universe make it a subject of ongoing interest and exploration for scientists and philosophers alike. As quantum computing and other quantum technologies continue to advance, the study of the Quantum Zeno effect is likely to become even more important and relevant.

CHAPTER 6.2: THE QUANTUM ZENO EFFECT AND CONSCIOUSNESS

The potential connection between the Quantum Zeno effect and consciousness has been a topic of discussion in both quantum mechanics and consciousness studies. While the idea that consciousness could play a role in the Quantum Zeno effect and the measurement problem remains controversial, some researchers have proposed that the phenomenon could be related to consciousness in various ways.

One proposed connection between the Quantum Zeno effect and consciousness is that the constant monitoring and observation of quantum systems by conscious beings could be responsible for the observed effects. This idea suggests that consciousness could actively interact with quantum systems and influence their evolution and behavior.

Another proposed connection is that the Quantum Zeno effect could be related to the concept of attention in consciousness. Attention is the process of focusing on a specific aspect of the environment or internal mental states, and it is known to have a powerful influence on our perception and behavior. Some researchers have suggested that attention could be related to the Quantum Zeno effect, as it involves the continuous observation and monitoring of a specific aspect of the environment or mental state.

However, the idea that consciousness alone can account for the Quantum Zeno effect and the measurement problem remains controversial. Many scientists and philosophers argue that other physical mechanisms, such as decoherence, may be responsible for these effects.

Nonetheless, the potential connection between the Quantum Zeno effect and consciousness continues to be an area of ongoing research and exploration. As our understanding of quantum mechanics and consciousness continues to evolve, we may gain a deeper understanding of the relationship between these two fundamental aspects of our world.

CHAPTER 6.3: EXPERIMENTAL EVIDENCE FOR THE QUANTUM ZENO EFFECT

The Quantum Zeno effect has been observed and studied in a variety of experimental settings, providing evidence for its existence and potential applications. One of the earliest and most well-known experiments demonstrating the Quantum Zeno effect involved the decay of an unstable particle, such as a neutron. By continuously measuring the particle's state, scientists were able to slow down or even prevent its decay, effectively "freezing" it in place.

Other experiments have demonstrated the Quantum Zeno effect in a variety of quantum systems, including trapped ions, superconducting qubits, and photon polarization states. These experiments have provided further evidence for the phenomenon and its potential applications in quantum information processing and quantum computing.

One exciting application of the Quantum Zeno effect is in quantum error correction. By continuously monitoring and measuring quantum systems, errors can be detected and corrected before they can cause significant damage to the system. This could be especially important in the development of practical quantum computers, where errors can be a significant challenge.

In addition to its potential applications, the Quantum Zeno effect also raises important questions about the fundamental nature of reality and the role of observation and measurement in quantum mechanics. While the exact mechanism behind the phenomenon remains a subject of ongoing research and debate, its experimental observation provides further evidence for the strange and fascinating behavior of quantum systems.

Moreover, the study of the Quantum Zeno effect also has significant implications for consciousness studies. The role of observation and measurement in the phenomenon raises questions about the potential relationship between consciousness and quantum mechanics. Some researchers have suggested that the Quantum Zeno effect provides evidence for the idea that consciousness plays a fundamental role in the collapse of the wave function, a key process in quantum mechanics.

However, this remains a controversial and heavily debated topic, with many scientists and philosophers arguing that consciousness is not necessary for the explanation of quantum phenomena. Regardless of the specific conclusions drawn, the study of the Quantum Zeno effect has opened up new avenues for exploring the relationship between consciousness and the quantum world.

Overall, the Quantum Zeno effect represents an important and intriguing phenomenon in both quantum mechanics and consciousness studies. Its potential applications in quantum information processing and quantum computing make it an area of significant interest for researchers and engineers, while its implications for our understanding of the fundamental nature of reality and the role of consciousness in quantum mechanics make it a fascinating topic for philosophers and theorists. As research in these areas continues to progress, we may gain even deeper insights into the mysterious and complex nature of the universe and the relationship between consciousness and the quantum world.

CHAPTER 7: QUANTUM MECHANICS AND THE MIND-BODY PROBLEM

One of the most fundamental questions in philosophy and psychology is the mind-body problem: how do our subjective experiences and consciousness relate to the physical world and the functioning of our brains? The advent of quantum mechanics has added a new layer of complexity to this question, as it suggests that the very nature of reality may be fundamentally different from what we have traditionally understood.

In this chapter, we will explore the implications of quantum mechanics for the mind-body problem and examine some of the major theories and debates in this area.

The Challenge of Consciousness in Science

Before we dive into the specifics of quantum mechanics and consciousness, it is important to acknowledge the challenge that consciousness poses to science in general. Consciousness is a subjective experience, and as such, it is not directly observable or measurable in the same way that physical phenomena are. This presents a significant challenge for scientists seeking to study consciousness and understand its relationship to the brain and the physical world.

Despite these challenges, scientists and philosophers have made significant progress in recent years in developing theories and models of consciousness that attempt to bridge the gap between subjective experience and objective measurement. The advent of quantum mechanics has added a new layer of complexity to these debates, as it suggests that the nature of reality may be inherently different from what we have traditionally understood.

Quantum Mechanics and the Nature of Reality

One of the key insights of quantum mechanics is that the act of observation and measurement can fundamentally alter the state of a quantum system. This is due to the wave-particle duality of quantum particles, which means that particles can exist as both waves and particles simultaneously and only collapse into a definite state upon measurement or observation.

This has led to a number of interpretations of quantum mechanics that have challenged our traditional understanding of the nature of reality. The Copenhagen interpretation, for example, suggests that the act of measurement creates the collapse of the wave function and therefore creates a definitive reality out of the range of possibilities that existed prior to measurement. The Many-Worlds interpretation, on the other hand, suggests that every possible outcome of a quantum measurement occurs in a separate parallel universe.

These interpretations have significant implications for our understanding of the mind-body problem, as they suggest that the act of observation and measurement may play a fundamental role in the creation of reality itself.

Theories of Quantum Consciousness

The relationship between quantum mechanics and consciousness has been the subject of much debate and speculation over the years. Some researchers have suggested that the fundamental nature of reality described by quantum mechanics provides a potential explanation for the subjective experience of consciousness. Others have argued that the complex and unpredictable nature of quantum mechanics makes it an unlikely candidate for explaining consciousness.

One popular theory of quantum consciousness is the Orchestrated Objective Reduction (Orch-OR) theory developed by physicist Roger Penrose and anesthesiologist Stuart Hameroff. This theory suggests that the collapse of the wave function is orchestrated by microtubules in the brain, which act as quantum computers and are responsible for generating conscious experience. However, this theory remains controversial and has not been widely accepted in the scientific community.

Other theories of quantum consciousness have focused on the potential role of entanglement and coherence in the brain, suggesting that these phenomena may play a role in the emergence of conscious experience. However, much more research is needed in this area to fully understand the potential relationship between quantum mechanics and consciousness.

Implications for the Mind-Body Problem

The relationship between quantum mechanics and the mind-body problem remains an area of ongoing research and debate. While some researchers have suggested that the strange and unpredictable nature of quantum mechanics provides a potential explanation for the subjective experience of consciousness, others have argued that the complex and multi-layered nature of consciousness makes it unlikely that quantum mechanics alone can account for it.

One potential avenue for exploring the relationship between quantum mechanics and consciousness is through the study of quantum brain dynamics. This field seeks to understand how quantum processes may be involved in the functioning of the brain, and how this could relate to conscious experience. Some researchers have proposed that quantum entanglement could play a role in the neural processes underlying consciousness, while others have suggested that the collapse of the wave function could be involved in decision-making processes.

However, there are also many challenges associated with this approach. For example, it is not yet clear whether quantum processes are actually present in the brain at the relevant scale and timescale required for conscious experience. Furthermore, even if quantum mechanics is involved in the brain, it remains to be seen how this could give rise to the complex and integrated nature of conscious experience.

Overall, the relationship between quantum mechanics and the mind-body problem is a complex and ongoing area of research. While there is still much to learn, the insights gained from quantum mechanics may ultimately shed light on some of the deepest mysteries of consciousness and the nature of reality itself.

CHAPTER 7.1: THE MIND-BODY PROBLEM AND ITS HISTORY

The mind-body problem has been a philosophical conundrum for centuries, dating back to the ancient Greeks. At its core, the problem concerns the relationship between the mind, which is typically associated with consciousness, and the body, which is typically associated with physical matter. The question is: how can these two fundamentally different aspects of reality be related to each other?

The history of the mind-body problem can be traced through the works of numerous philosophers and thinkers, each with their own take on the issue. One of the earliest and most influential was René Descartes, who proposed a dualistic view of reality in which the mind and body were separate substances that interacted with each other. Descartes believed that the mind was immaterial and could exist independently of the body, and that the body was merely a machine that could be studied through the methods of science.

Other philosophers, such as Baruch Spinoza and Gottfried Leibniz, rejected Descartes' dualism and proposed a monistic view of reality, in which the mind and body were different aspects of the same fundamental substance. Immanuel Kant later introduced the concept of the noumenon and the phenomenon, arguing that the mind and the body could not be fully understood through empirical observation alone.

In the 20th century, the mind-body problem became even more

complex with the rise of quantum mechanics. The principles of quantum mechanics, such as superposition and entanglement, challenged traditional views of reality and led some researchers to explore the possibility of a quantum theory of consciousness.

Today, the mind-body problem remains a topic of intense debate and research, with various theories and models proposed to explain the relationship between the mind and the body. Some researchers have suggested that consciousness arises from the complexity of neural networks in the brain, while others have proposed a non-local or even spiritual dimension to consciousness.

As we explore the implications of quantum mechanics on the mind-body problem, it is important to keep in mind the rich and complex history of this philosophical conundrum. By understanding the ideas and arguments that have been put forth over the centuries, we can better appreciate the challenges and opportunities that lie ahead in our quest to understand the nature of consciousness and the relationship between mind and matter.

Another important figure in the history of the mind-body problem is Immanuel Kant, a German philosopher who lived in the 18th century. Kant argued that the mind and body are fundamentally different, but that they are also interconnected and interdependent. According to Kant, the mind is responsible for organizing sensory data and creating our experience of the world, while the body provides the raw material for this experience.

In the 20th century, a number of philosophers and scientists began to challenge traditional views of the mind-body problem, leading to new theories and perspectives on the nature of consciousness and the relationship between mind and matter. One influential idea is known as functionalism, which suggests that mental states can be defined in terms of their functional roles or relationships to other mental states and to behavior. Another important perspective is embodied cognition, which emphasizes the ways in which our physical bodies and environments shape and influence our thoughts and experiences.

The advent of quantum mechanics has added another layer of complexity to the mind-body problem, as scientists and philosophers grapple with the implications of quantum phenomena such as entanglement, superposition, and non-locality. Some theorists have suggested that these quantum effects could help to explain the mysterious nature of consciousness, while others remain skeptical of such claims.

As we continue to explore the mind-body problem in light of quantum mechanics and other new developments in science and philosophy, it is clear that there is still much we do not know or understand about the nature of consciousness and the relationship between mind and matter. Nevertheless, the pursuit of this knowledge remains a fascinating and important endeavor, with profound implications for our understanding of ourselves and our place in the world.

CHAPTER 7.2: HOW QUANTUM MECHANICS CAN HELP SOLVE THE MIND-BODY PROBLEM

The mind-body problem has puzzled philosophers for centuries, and attempts to solve it have ranged from the dualist views of Descartes to the functionalist and embodied perspectives of modern times. However, the advent of quantum mechanics has opened up new avenues for exploring this problem, and many theorists have suggested that quantum phenomena could hold the key to understanding the nature of consciousness and the relationship between mind and matter.

One way in which quantum mechanics could help to solve the mind-body problem is by shedding light on the mysterious nature of consciousness itself. According to some theorists, the complex and unpredictable behavior of quantum systems could be seen as a metaphor for the workings of the human mind, with consciousness emerging from the entangled and superimposed states of subatomic particles.

For example, the phenomenon of entanglement, in which two particles become correlated in such a way that their states cannot be described independently, has been suggested as a possible explanation for the unity and coherence of conscious experience. If consciousness arises from the entangled states of neural activity in the brain, then it could be argued that the mind and body are inextricably linked in a way that cannot be reduced to purely physical processes.

Similarly, the concept of superposition, in which a particle exists in multiple states simultaneously, could be seen as a way of explaining the multiple perspectives and subjective experiences that make up our conscious awareness. If consciousness arises from the combination of many possible states or "wave functions" of neural activity, then it could be argued that the mind is a quantum phenomenon that cannot be fully understood in terms of classical physics.

Of course, these ideas remain highly speculative, and many scientists and philosophers remain skeptical of claims that quantum mechanics can help to solve the mind-body problem. Some have argued that the brain is simply too warm and noisy an environment for quantum effects to play a significant role, while others have suggested that even if quantum phenomena are involved in consciousness, they may not be sufficient to explain the full range of human experience.

Nevertheless, the exploration of the relationship between quantum mechanics and consciousness remains an exciting and rapidly developing field, with many researchers working to uncover the mechanisms by which quantum phenomena could contribute to conscious awareness. Whether or not quantum mechanics can ultimately help to solve the mind-body problem, it is clear that the study of quantum consciousness has the potential to revolutionize our understanding of ourselves and our place in the universe.

CHAPTER 7.3: OBJECTIONS TO QUANTUM MECHANICS AS A SOLUTION TO THE MIND-BODY PROBLEM

While some theorists have suggested that quantum mechanics could hold the key to solving the mind-body problem, others remain skeptical of this approach. In this chapter, we will explore some of the objections that have been raised against the idea that quantum mechanics can help to explain consciousness and the relationship between mind and matter.

One common objection is that the brain is simply too large and warm a system for quantum effects to play a significant role in consciousness. According to this view, the noise and thermal fluctuations of the brain's environment would quickly "decohere" any quantum states, making it unlikely that quantum mechanics could be responsible for the complex and coherent nature of conscious experience.

Furthermore, some theorists argue that even if quantum mechanics does play a role in consciousness, it is unlikely to be sufficient to explain the full range of human experience. For example, while entanglement and superposition may be able to explain certain aspects of conscious awareness, they may not be able to account for the complexity and richness of our emotions, thoughts, and perceptions.

Another objection to the quantum approach to the mind-body problem is that it relies on a certain level of anthropomorphism, or the attribution of human-like qualities to non-human systems. While quantum mechanics may be an accurate description of subatomic particles, it is not clear that it can be extended to more complex systems such as the brain and consciousness without making assumptions about their nature and properties.

Finally, some critics have pointed out that the idea of quantum consciousness may simply be an example of "woo-woo" or pseudoscientific thinking, with little empirical evidence to support its claims. While some studies have suggested a possible connection between quantum effects and consciousness, many of these findings remain controversial and have yet to be replicated by independent researchers.

In conclusion, while the idea of quantum consciousness has captured the imagination of many scientists and philosophers, it remains a highly controversial and speculative area of research. While it is possible that quantum mechanics could provide new insights into the mind-body problem, it is also important to remain skeptical of claims that cannot be supported by rigorous empirical evidence and sound scientific reasoning. Ultimately, the pursuit of knowledge in this area will require a careful and interdisciplinary approach that combines insights from physics, neuroscience, philosophy, and psychology.

CHAPTER 8: QUANTUM NONLOCALITY AND CONSCIOUSNESS

The phenomenon of quantum nonlocality is one of the most intriguing and puzzling aspects of quantum mechanics. It refers to the ability of particles to become instantaneously correlated in such a way that their states cannot be described independently, regardless of the distance between them. This phenomenon challenges our intuitive notions of causality and locality, and has led some theorists to suggest that it could be relevant to understanding the nature of consciousness.

In this chapter, we will explore the relationship between quantum nonlocality and consciousness, and consider some of the implications of this connection.

One way in which quantum nonlocality could be relevant to consciousness is through the idea of "spooky action at a distance," as famously described by Einstein, Podolsky, and Rosen in their 1935 paper. According to this idea, entangled particles can become instantaneously correlated, even if they are separated by vast distances, in a way that violates the principle of locality. This has led some theorists to suggest that the brain, which is composed of many particles, could be capable of "quantum entanglement" with other systems in the universe, including other brains or even the entire cosmos.

If this is true, it could provide a new way of understanding the interconnectedness of all things, and suggest that consciousness is not simply an individual phenomenon but is, in fact, part of a larger and more fundamental aspect of reality.

Another way in which quantum nonlocality could be relevant to consciousness is through the idea of "quantum coherence." Coherence refers to the ability of particles to maintain a stable and correlated state over time, and is thought to be necessary for quantum phenomena such as entanglement and superposition. If consciousness arises from the coherent states of neural activity in the brain, as some theorists have suggested, then it could be argued that quantum nonlocality is a necessary condition for the emergence of conscious experience.

Furthermore, the idea of quantum nonlocality could help to explain certain aspects of consciousness that are difficult to reconcile with classical physics. For example, the unity and coherence of conscious experience, as well as the subjective nature of perception and thought, could be seen as emerging from the entangled and superimposed states of quantum systems.

However, it is important to note that the idea of quantum nonlocality and consciousness remains highly speculative, and many scientists and philosophers remain skeptical of these claims. While there is evidence to suggest that quantum phenomena play a role in some aspects of biological processes, it is not yet clear whether they are relevant to the emergence of consciousness.

In conclusion, the study of quantum nonlocality and consciousness remains an exciting and rapidly developing field, with many researchers working to uncover the mechanisms by which quantum phenomena could contribute to conscious awareness. Whether or not quantum nonlocality is ultimately found to be relevant to consciousness, it is clear that the pursuit of knowledge in this area has the potential to revolutionize our understanding of ourselves and our place in the universe.

CHAPTER 8.1: DEFINITION OF NONLOCALITY

In quantum mechanics, nonlocality refers to the phenomenon in which particles become instantaneously correlated in such a way that their states cannot be described independently, regardless of the distance between them. This means that the behavior of one particle can instantaneously affect the behavior of another particle, even if they are separated by vast distances.

Nonlocality arises from the fact that particles can become "entangled," meaning that their properties become correlated in such a way that they cannot be described independently. For example, two particles could become entangled in such a way that the spin of one particle is always opposite to the spin of the other particle, regardless of the distance between them.

The implications of nonlocality are profound, as they challenge our intuitive notions of causality and locality. Nonlocality suggests that the universe is fundamentally interconnected in a way that cannot be described by classical physics, and that the behavior of one system can be influenced by another system, even if they are separated by vast distances.

Nonlocality is a necessary condition for some of the most intriguing and mysterious phenomena in quantum mechanics, including entanglement, superposition, and quantum teleportation. These phenomena have led some theorists to suggest that nonlocality could be relevant to understanding the nature of consciousness, and to exploring the possibility of quantum cognition.

However, it is important to note that the phenomenon of nonlocality remains a subject of active debate and research in the field of quantum mechanics. While there is evidence to suggest that nonlocality plays a role in some aspects of biological processes, it is not yet clear whether it is relevant to the emergence of consciousness.

In the next section, we will explore some of the ways in which nonlocality could be relevant to understanding the role of nonlocality in consciousness.

CHAPTER 8.2: THE ROLE OF NONLOCALITY IN CONSCIOUSNESS

The relationship between nonlocality and consciousness has been a topic of speculation and debate among researchers and theorists for decades. Some have suggested that nonlocality could be a key factor in explaining the mysterious and elusive nature of consciousness, while others remain skeptical of such claims.

One of the most intriguing theories linking nonlocality and consciousness is the idea of quantum entanglement between neurons in the brain. According to this theory, neurons could become entangled in such a way that their states are nonlocal, meaning that they cannot be described independently of each other. This could allow for the creation of highly coherent and synchronized patterns of neural activity, which could be related to the emergence of conscious experience.

Another theory linking nonlocality and consciousness is the idea of quantum computation in the brain. According to this theory, the brain could perform certain types of computations using quantum processes, which could allow for faster and more efficient information processing than classical processes. Nonlocality would be a necessary component of such processes, as it would allow for the synchronization and coordination of quantum states across different parts of the brain.

However, there are also several objections to the idea that nonlocality plays a significant role in consciousness. One objection is that the effects of nonlocality are typically very small and difficult to observe, making it unlikely that they could play a major role in brain function. Additionally, the idea that the brain performs quantum computations is still a matter of debate among researchers, and it is not yet clear how such processes could give rise to conscious experience.

Despite these objections, the idea that nonlocality could be relevant to understanding consciousness remains an intriguing and active area of research. Advances in technology and experimental techniques are allowing researchers to investigate the role of nonlocality in biological systems with increasing precision, and it is possible that new insights into the nature of consciousness will emerge from these investigations.

CHAPTER 8.3: EXPERIMENTAL EVIDENCE FOR QUANTUM NONLOCALITY

While the concept of nonlocality may seem strange and counterintuitive, there is a wealth of experimental evidence supporting its existence. In this section, we will explore some of the most compelling experiments that have demonstrated the reality of nonlocality, and discuss their implications for our understanding of quantum mechanics and consciousness.

One of the most famous experiments demonstrating nonlocality is the EPR (Einstein-Podolsky-Rosen) experiment. In this experiment, two particles (typically photons) are created in such a way that their states are entangled. This means that their properties, such as spin or polarization, become correlated in such a way that they cannot be described independently of each other.

The EPR experiment involves measuring the spin of one of the particles, which causes the other particle to instantaneously "collapse" into a corresponding spin state, even if it is located on the other side of the universe. This instant correlation between the two particles violates our classical notions of causality and locality, and provides strong evidence for the reality of nonlocality.

Another experiment that has provided evidence for nonlocality is the Bell test. The Bell test involves creating pairs of entangled particles and measuring their states in different directions. The results of these measurements are then compared to the predictions of classical physics.

According to classical physics, the correlations between the two particles should be limited by a certain value known as "Bell's inequality." However, experiments have shown that the actual correlations between entangled particles can exceed Bell's inequality, providing strong evidence for the reality of nonlocality.

In recent years, advances in technology have allowed researchers to conduct increasingly sophisticated experiments to explore the phenomenon of nonlocality. For example, experiments using entangled photons have demonstrated that nonlocality can be observed over distances of several kilometers, and have even demonstrated the possibility of "teleporting" quantum states from one location to another.

Other experiments have investigated the possibility of nonlocality in biological systems. For example, researchers have measured the spin of electrons in photosynthetic pigments and have observed nonlocal correlations between the spins of these electrons, suggesting that nonlocality may play a role in the efficiency of photosynthesis.

While these experiments provide compelling evidence for the reality of nonlocality, they also raise a number of philosophical and theoretical questions. For example, nonlocality challenges our classical notions of causality and locality, suggesting that the universe may be fundamentally interconnected in a way that cannot be described by classical physics.

Additionally, the phenomenon of nonlocality raises questions about the relationship between mind and matter. Some theorists have suggested that the existence of nonlocal correlations between particles could be relevant to understanding the nature of consciousness, and to exploring the possibility of quantum cognition.

However, it is important to note that the implications of

nonlocality for consciousness are still a matter of debate and speculation among researchers. While there is evidence to suggest that nonlocality plays a role in some aspects of biological processes, it is not yet clear whether it is relevant to the emergence of consciousness.

Furthermore, the interpretation of quantum mechanics that underlies the phenomenon of nonlocality, known as the "Copenhagen interpretation," remains a subject of controversy among physicists and philosophers. Some researchers have suggested alternative interpretations of quantum mechanics, such as the "many worlds" interpretation, which do not involve nonlocality.

Despite these challenges, the experimental evidence for nonlocality remains one of the most intriguing and mysterious aspects of quantum mechanics. The existence of nonlocal correlations between particles challenges our classical intuitions about the nature of reality, and raises profound questions about the relationship between mind and matter.

In conclusion, the phenomenon of nonlocality is one of the most profound and intriguing aspects of quantum mechanics. Its existence challenges our classical understanding of causality and locality, and raises important questions about the nature of consciousness and the relationship between mind and matter. While the experimental evidence for nonlocality is strong, its implications for consciousness remain a subject of debate and speculation.

Nonetheless, the study of nonlocality continues to be an active area of research, with new experiments and theoretical developments constantly emerging. As our understanding of quantum mechanics deepens, we may gain new insights into the nature of nonlocality and its potential role in biological and cognitive processes.

Ultimately, the exploration of nonlocality represents a

fascinating and important intersection between physics, philosophy, and neuroscience. By probing the mysteries of the quantum world, we may gain new perspectives on the nature of reality and the workings of the human mind.

CHAPTER 9: QUANTUM BIOLOGY

Quantum mechanics has revolutionized the way we think about the fundamental nature of reality. It has challenged our understanding of the physical world, showing us that the world we perceive is not necessarily the world that exists. Quantum mechanics has also challenged our traditional notions of causality, determinism, and objectivity, and introduced a new way of understanding the world in terms of probabilities, wave-particle duality, and non-locality.

In recent years, quantum mechanics has also made significant contributions to the study of biology. Quantum biology is a relatively new field that explores the intersection of quantum mechanics and biology, and seeks to understand how quantum mechanics might influence biological systems and processes.

One of the most exciting aspects of quantum biology is its potential to shed light on some of the most puzzling and enigmatic phenomena in biology, such as the process of photosynthesis, the workings of enzymes, and the behavior of biomolecules. In this chapter, we will explore some of the most exciting discoveries in quantum biology, and how they might inform our understanding of consciousness.

Photosynthesis

> Photosynthesis is the process by which plants and other photosynthetic organisms convert sunlight into energy. It is one of the most important processes on Earth, as it forms the basis of the food chain and is responsible for the majority of

the oxygen in the Earth's atmosphere.

For many years, scientists struggled to understand how photosynthesis worked at the molecular level. However, in the 1990s, researchers discovered that photosynthesis makes use of quantum coherence to efficiently transfer energy from the light-absorbing pigments to the reaction center where it can be used to drive chemical reactions.

Quantum coherence is a phenomenon in which a system of particles behaves as if it were a single entity, rather than a collection of individual particles. In the case of photosynthesis, the light-absorbing pigments act together to form a coherent state, which allows them to efficiently transfer energy to the reaction center. This coherence allows the energy to be transferred with very little loss or dissipation, which makes photosynthesis incredibly efficient.

The discovery of quantum coherence in photosynthesis is significant because it challenges our traditional understanding of how biological systems work. It suggests that biological systems might be making use of quantum mechanical processes to achieve their functions, rather than relying solely on classical physics.

Enzymes

Enzymes are biological molecules that catalyze chemical reactions in the body. They are essential for many biological processes, such as digestion, metabolism, and DNA replication.

For many years, scientists believed that enzymes worked like lock and key, where the enzyme would bind to a substrate molecule like a key fitting into a lock. However, in the past decade, researchers have discovered that enzymes might be using quantum tunneling to enhance their catalytic power.

Quantum tunneling is a phenomenon in which a particle can pass through a potential barrier even if it does not have enough energy to do so classically. In the case of enzymes, researchers have found evidence that hydrogen atoms can tunnel through energy barriers to reach the active site of the enzyme, where they can participate in chemical reactions.

The discovery of quantum tunneling in enzymes is significant because it suggests that enzymes might be using quantum mechanics to overcome the energetic barriers that would normally prevent chemical reactions from occurring. This discovery also has implications for the design of new drugs and catalysts, as it suggests that quantum tunneling might be a powerful tool for enhancing catalytic activity.

Biomolecules

Biomolecules are the building blocks of life, and they include molecules such as DNA, proteins, and carbohydrates. The behavior of biomolecules is one of the most important and complex areas of biology, as it determines the structure and function of cells and organisms.

In recent years, researchers have discovered that biomolecules might be making use of quantum mechanics to achieve their functions. One of the most significant examples of this is the phenomenon of quantum entanglement, where two particles become inextricably linked, so that any change in one particle instantaneously affects the other particle, no matter how far apart they are.

Recent studies have shown that quantum entanglement may play a role in the functioning of proteins. Proteins are complex biomolecules that are responsible for a wide range of biological functions, from catalyzing chemical reactions to transporting molecules across cell membranes.

Researchers have found that certain proteins exhibit quantum entanglement, which may help to explain their remarkable stability and ability to function in a variety of environments. Additionally, the discovery of quantum entanglement in biomolecules has opened up new avenues for understanding the relationship between quantum mechanics and biological systems.

Quantum Consciousness

The discovery of quantum coherence, quantum tunneling, and quantum entanglement in biological systems has led some researchers to speculate about the role of quantum mechanics in consciousness.

One of the most intriguing ideas in this area is the concept of quantum cognition, which proposes that the brain might be making use of quantum mechanics to perform certain cognitive functions. For example, some researchers have suggested that the brain might be using quantum entanglement to perform rapid computations or to store and retrieve memories.

The idea of quantum consciousness has also been proposed, which suggests that consciousness might be a quantum phenomenon. Some proponents of this idea suggest that consciousness arises from the interaction between classical and quantum processes in the brain.

While the idea of quantum consciousness is still controversial and debated in the scientific community, it raises some interesting questions about the relationship between quantum mechanics and consciousness. It also highlights the need for further research in this area to fully understand the potential role of quantum mechanics in biological systems and consciousness.

Conclusion

Quantum biology is a rapidly growing field that is opening up new avenues for understanding the fundamental processes of life. The discovery of quantum coherence, quantum tunneling, and quantum entanglement in biological systems has challenged our traditional understanding of how biological systems work and has opened up new possibilities for the design of new drugs and catalysts.

While the idea of quantum consciousness is still in its infancy, it raises some interesting questions about the relationship between quantum mechanics and consciousness. As researchers continue to explore the intersection of quantum mechanics and biology, we may gain new insights into the nature of life and consciousness, and perhaps even uncover new ways to enhance our understanding and control of these fundamental processes.

CHAPTER 9.1: THE EMERGENCE OF QUANTUM BIOLOGY

The field of quantum biology is a relatively new area of research that seeks to understand how biological systems make use of quantum mechanics. Although the field is still in its early stages, it has already provided some intriguing insights into the fundamental processes of life.

The Emergence of Quantum Biology

The idea that quantum mechanics might play a role in biological systems was first proposed in the 1930s by physicist Erwin Schrödinger. In his book "What is Life?" Schrödinger suggested that the fundamental properties of quantum mechanics, such as superposition and entanglement, might be involved in the processes of DNA replication and protein synthesis.

However, the idea of quantum mechanics in biology was largely dismissed by mainstream biologists and physicists, who believed that biological systems were too large and too warm to exhibit quantum behavior.

It was not until the 1990s that the field of quantum biology began to emerge as a serious area of research. One of the key developments was the discovery of quantum coherence in photosynthesis, which suggested that plants might be using quantum mechanics to achieve the high efficiency of energy transfer that is observed in photosynthesis.

Since then, researchers have discovered that biomolecules might be making use of other quantum phenomena, such as quantum tunneling and entanglement, to achieve their functions. This has led to a growing interest in the intersection of quantum mechanics and biology, and the development of a new field of research known as quantum biology.

Quantum Coherence

> One of the key concepts in quantum biology is quantum coherence, which refers to the phenomenon where particles can exist in multiple states simultaneously. In biological systems, quantum coherence has been observed in photosynthesis, where it is thought to play a crucial role in the efficient transfer of energy from light-harvesting pigments to the reaction center.
>
> In photosynthesis, light is absorbed by pigment molecules called chromophores, which then transfer the energy to neighboring chromophores until it reaches the reaction center. The efficiency of this energy transfer is believed to be due to quantum coherence, which allows the energy to exist in multiple states simultaneously and therefore explore all possible pathways for transfer.
>
> The discovery of quantum coherence in photosynthesis has sparked interest in the possibility of using quantum coherence to design more efficient solar cells and other energy-related technologies.

Quantum Tunneling

> Another quantum phenomenon that has been observed in biological systems is quantum tunneling, which refers to the ability of particles to tunnel through energy barriers that they would not be able to overcome classically.
>
> In biological systems, quantum tunneling has been observed in enzyme-catalyzed reactions, where it is thought to play

a crucial role in increasing the efficiency of the reaction. Enzymes are proteins that catalyze chemical reactions by lowering the activation energy required for the reaction to occur.

Quantum tunneling allows the reactant to tunnel through the activation energy barrier, rather than having to climb over it, which can significantly increase the rate of the reaction.

The discovery of quantum tunneling in enzymes has led to the development of new strategies for designing more efficient catalysts and drugs.

Quantum Entanglement

Perhaps the most intriguing quantum phenomenon observed in biological systems is quantum entanglement, where two particles become inextricably linked, so that any change in one particle instantaneously affects the other particle, no matter how far apart they are.

In biological systems, quantum entanglement has been observed in certain proteins, where it is thought to play a role in their remarkable stability and ability to function in a variety of environments.

The discovery of quantum entanglement in biomolecules has opened up new avenues for understanding the relationship between quantum mechanics and biological systems.

Conclusion

The emergence of quantum biology as a field of research has provided some intriguing insights into the fundamental processes of life. The discovery of quantum coherence, quantum tunneling, and quantum entanglement in biological systems has challenged the traditional view that biological systems are too large and too warm to exhibit quantum behavior. Instead, it suggests that biological systems might be exploiting the strange and counterintuitive properties of quantum mechanics to achieve their functions.

The implications of quantum biology for our understanding of consciousness are still largely unknown, but the idea that quantum mechanics might play a role in the brain has led to the development of the field of quantum consciousness. This field seeks to understand how the principles of quantum mechanics might be involved in consciousness and the subjective experience of the world.

Although the relationship between quantum mechanics and consciousness is still largely speculative, the emergence of quantum biology as a field of research provides a promising avenue for exploring this relationship. By understanding how biological systems make use of quantum mechanics, we might gain new insights into the mysterious nature of consciousness and the mind.

In conclusion, the emergence of quantum biology is a fascinating development in our understanding of the fundamental processes of life. It challenges our traditional view of biological systems and opens up new avenues for research into the relationship between quantum mechanics and consciousness. While the implications of quantum biology for consciousness are still largely unknown, the field provides an exciting opportunity for interdisciplinary collaboration and exploration.

CHAPTER 9.2: QUANTUM BIOLOGY AND CONSCIOUSNESS

The relationship between quantum biology and consciousness is a topic of growing interest and speculation. While the implications of quantum biology for consciousness are still largely unknown, the idea that quantum mechanics might play a role in the brain has led to the development of the field of quantum consciousness.

The Brain as a Quantum System

The brain is a complex network of neurons and synapses that process and transmit information throughout the body. While classical physics provides a good description of the behavior of macroscopic objects, it fails to explain the behavior of individual particles at the quantum level. However, recent studies have suggested that certain aspects of brain function might be better explained by quantum mechanics.

For example, some researchers have proposed that quantum tunneling might play a role in the communication between neurons, which could explain the high speed and efficiency of neural communication. Others have suggested that quantum coherence might be involved in the processing and storage of information in the brain.

One of the most intriguing proposals is that the phenomenon of quantum entanglement might be involved in consciousness. This idea suggests that the entanglement of particles in the brain might give rise to the subjective experience of consciousness.

Quantum Entanglement and Consciousness

Quantum entanglement is a phenomenon where two particles become inextricably linked, so that any change in one particle instantaneously affects the other particle, no matter how far apart they are. This strange and counterintuitive phenomenon has been observed in a variety of physical systems, including biological systems.

The idea that quantum entanglement might be involved in consciousness is based on the idea that the subjective experience of consciousness arises from the integration of information across different parts of the brain. This integration might be achieved through the entanglement of particles in the brain.

The theory suggests that the subjective experience of consciousness arises from the interaction of entangled particles in the brain, which gives rise to the perception of a unified and coherent reality. In other words, the experience of consciousness might be a manifestation of the entanglement of particles in the brain.

Critiques and Challenges

While the idea of quantum consciousness is intriguing, it is still a highly speculative theory that is subject to critique and challenge. One of the key criticisms of the theory is that quantum mechanics is typically only observed at very small scales, and it is unclear whether it would be observable at the scale of the brain.

Another challenge to the theory is that the effects of quantum mechanics are typically very short-lived, and it is unclear how such effects could give rise to the sustained and stable experience of consciousness.

Despite these critiques and challenges, the idea of quantum consciousness continues to generate interest and speculation in the fields of neuroscience and quantum physics.

Conclusion

The relationship between quantum biology and consciousness is still largely speculative, but the emergence of the field of quantum biology provides a promising avenue for exploring this relationship. By understanding how biological systems make use of quantum mechanics, we might gain new insights into the mysterious nature of consciousness and the mind.

While the idea of quantum consciousness is still highly speculative, it provides a fascinating and thought-provoking theory about the relationship between quantum mechanics and consciousness. The idea that consciousness might arise from the entanglement of particles in the brain challenges our traditional view of consciousness as a purely classical phenomenon, and opens up new avenues for interdisciplinary research and exploration.

As the field of quantum biology continues to develop, it is likely that we will gain new insights into the relationship between quantum mechanics and consciousness. While the ultimate implications of this relationship are still unknown, the field provides an exciting opportunity for interdisciplinary collaboration and exploration.

CHAPTER 9.3: THE FUTURE OF QUANTUM BIOLOGY AND CONSCIOUSNESS STUDIES

The field of quantum biology is still in its infancy, but it has already provided some intriguing insights into the fundamental processes of life. As the field continues to develop, it is likely that we will gain new insights into the relationship between quantum mechanics and consciousness.

One of the most exciting developments in the field of quantum biology is the use of quantum technologies to study biological systems. These technologies allow us to probe biological systems at the quantum level and to observe quantum behavior in living systems.

For example, researchers have used superposition and entanglement to study the behavior of photosynthetic complexes in plants and bacteria, and have discovered that these complexes might be using quantum coherence to achieve their function. Other researchers have used quantum tunneling to study the transport of electrons in enzymes and proteins, and have discovered that these processes might be more efficient than classical models would suggest.

The use of quantum technologies in biological research is still in its early stages, but it provides a promising avenue for future research into the relationship between quantum mechanics and biology.

The Future of Quantum Consciousness Studies

The field of quantum consciousness is still highly speculative, but it has already generated interest and debate in the fields of neuroscience and quantum physics. As the field continues to develop, it is likely that we will gain new insights into the relationship between quantum mechanics and consciousness.

One of the most promising avenues for future research is the study of the brain as a quantum system. Researchers are exploring the idea that the brain might be using quantum mechanics to achieve its functions, and are developing new technologies to study the brain at the quantum level.

For example, researchers are using magnetic resonance imaging (MRI) to study the quantum properties of the brain, and are developing new techniques for measuring the coherence of neural networks. Other researchers are using quantum technologies to study the properties of individual neurons and synapses, and to explore the role of quantum coherence in neural communication.

As the field of quantum consciousness continues to develop, it is likely that we will gain new insights into the nature of consciousness and the mind. While the idea of quantum consciousness is still highly speculative, it provides an exciting and thought-provoking theory about the relationship between quantum mechanics and consciousness.

Conclusion

The emergence of quantum biology as a field of research has challenged our traditional view of biological systems and opened up new avenues for exploring the relationship between quantum mechanics and consciousness. While the implications of quantum biology for consciousness are still largely unknown, the field provides an exciting opportunity for interdisciplinary collaboration and exploration.

The study of quantum consciousness is still highly speculative, but it has already generated interest and debate in the fields of neuroscience and quantum physics. As the field continues to develop, it is likely that we will gain new insights into the nature of consciousness and the mind.

In conclusion, the fields of quantum biology and quantum consciousness provide promising avenues for future research and exploration. By understanding how biological systems make use of quantum mechanics, and by exploring the relationship between quantum mechanics and consciousness, we might gain new insights into the mysterious nature of life and consciousness.

CHAPTER 10: QUANTUM INFORMATION PROCESSING IN THE BRAIN

The brain is arguably the most complex and mysterious organ in the human body. It is responsible for everything from our thoughts and emotions to our movements and sensations. Scientists have been studying the brain for centuries, yet we still have much to learn about its inner workings.

In recent years, there has been growing interest in the idea that the brain might be using quantum mechanics to process information. This idea is based on the fact that many of the processes in the brain involve the movement of charged particles, which can exhibit quantum behavior under certain conditions.

The study of quantum information processing in the brain is still in its early stages, but it has already generated interest and debate in the fields of neuroscience and quantum physics. In this chapter, we will explore the concept of quantum information processing in the brain, and what it might mean for our understanding of consciousness.

What is Quantum Information Processing?

Quantum information processing refers to the use of quantum mechanics to process and manipulate information. In classical information processing, information is encoded in bits, which can take on one of two values (0 or 1). In quantum information processing, information is encoded in quantum bits (qubits), which can take on an infinite number of values due to their ability to exist in a superposition of states.

One of the most powerful features of quantum information processing is quantum entanglement. This phenomenon occurs when two particles become linked in such a way that the state of one particle is dependent on the state of the other, even when they are physically separated. This allows for the creation of highly secure communication systems, as any attempt to intercept or eavesdrop on the communication would disturb the entangled particles and be immediately detectable.

Quantum Information Processing in the Brain

The idea of quantum information processing in the brain is based on the fact that many of the processes in the brain involve the movement of charged particles, such as ions and electrons. These particles can exhibit quantum behavior under certain conditions, and it is possible that the brain might be using this quantum behavior to process information.

One area of the brain that has been proposed as a potential site for quantum information processing is the microtubules in neurons. Microtubules are hollow tubes made of protein that form the structural backbone of the neuron. They are also involved in the transport of molecules and organelles within the neuron.

The theory of quantum information processing in the brain proposes that the microtubules in neurons might be using quantum coherence to achieve their functions. Specifically, the theory proposes that the microtubules might be using entanglement to synchronize the activity of neurons and to process information in a highly efficient manner.

Evidence for Quantum Information Processing in the Brain

The idea of quantum information processing in the brain is still highly speculative, and there is currently limited evidence to support the theory. However, there have been some intriguing findings that suggest that quantum processes might be occurring in the brain.

One of the most compelling pieces of evidence comes from the study of photosynthesis in plants. Researchers have discovered that the process of photosynthesis involves the use of quantum coherence to achieve its function. Specifically, the plant uses quantum coherence to transport energy from the chlorophyll molecules to the reaction center, where the energy is used to drive the process of photosynthesis.

While photosynthesis is a process that occurs in plants, it is possible that similar processes are occurring in the brain. If the brain is indeed using quantum coherence to process information, it is possible that this could explain some of the mysterious properties of consciousness, such as its ability to integrate information from multiple sources and to generate novel insights and ideas.

Future Directions in the Study of Quantum Information Processing in the Brain

The study of quantum information processing in the brain is still in its early stages, and there is much work to be done to fully understand the role of quantum mechanics in the brain. Here are some potential avenues for future research:

1. Further exploration of microtubules: While microtubules have been proposed as a potential site for quantum information processing in the brain, there is still much to learn about their role in neural function. Future studies could explore the specific properties of microtubules that might enable quantum coherence and entanglement.
2. Experimental evidence: Currently, much of the evidence for quantum information processing in the brain is theoretical. Future studies could focus on developing experimental techniques to directly observe and measure quantum behavior in neurons.
3. Integration with neuroscience: In order to fully understand the role of quantum mechanics in the brain, it will be important to integrate the study of quantum information processing with traditional neuroscience research. This could involve collaborations between physicists and neuroscientists, or the development of interdisciplinary research teams.
4. Application to artificial intelligence: The field of artificial intelligence has made significant progress in recent years, but there are still limitations to the traditional algorithms used in machine learning. The use of quantum information processing could potentially lead to the development of more efficient and powerful algorithms for AI.

Conclusion

The study of quantum information processing in the brain is a fascinating and rapidly evolving field. While there is currently limited evidence to support the idea that the brain is using quantum mechanics to process information, the potential implications for our understanding of consciousness and neural function are significant.

Future research in this field could shed light on some of the mysteries of the brain and could potentially lead to the development of new technologies and therapies for neurological disorders. As we continue to explore the relationship between quantum mechanics and the brain, we may come to a deeper understanding of the complex interplay between physics and biology in the formation of consciousness.

CHAPTER 10.1: THE ROLE OF QUANTUM INFORMATION PROCESSING IN THE BRAIN

> The human brain is one of the most complex and sophisticated structures in the known universe. It is capable of performing numerous tasks simultaneously, ranging from conscious thought to regulating the body's vital functions. For many years, scientists have been fascinated by the brain's abilities and have tried to understand the mechanisms underlying its operation.

The recent development of quantum information processing (QIP) has provided new insights into the brain's workings, suggesting that quantum mechanics may play a crucial role in cognitive processes. In this chapter, we will explore the role of QIP in the brain and its potential implications for our understanding of consciousness.

The Role of Neurons

> To understand how quantum mechanics might play a role in the brain, it is helpful to first consider the basic building blocks of the brain: neurons. Neurons are specialized cells that transmit information through electrical and chemical signals. These signals are generated by the movement of charged particles across the cell membrane and the release of neurotransmitters at the synapses, the junctions between neurons.

> The behavior of neurons has traditionally been described

using classical physics. However, recent research suggests that quantum mechanics may be involved in the processes underlying neuronal communication. In particular, the behavior of the ion channels in the cell membrane that regulate the flow of ions into and out of the neuron may be governed by quantum effects. These channels act like tiny switches that can be turned on or off, allowing ions to flow into or out of the neuron. Quantum mechanics may play a role in this process by allowing the ions to tunnel through the channel barriers, which would otherwise be impossible according to classical physics.

The Role of Entanglement

Another aspect of QIP that may be relevant to the brain is entanglement. Entanglement is a quantum phenomenon in which two or more particles become correlated in such a way that the state of one particle depends on the state of the other particle, even if they are separated by large distances. This effect has been observed in experiments with particles such as photons and electrons.

In recent years, researchers have proposed that entanglement may play a role in neural communication. The idea is that the entanglement of particles in the brain could allow for more efficient and robust communication between neurons. In this model, the state of one neuron would be entangled with the state of another neuron, allowing for instantaneous communication between the two.

While the idea of entanglement playing a role in the brain is intriguing, there is currently little direct evidence to support it. It is also unclear how such entanglement would be created and maintained in the brain, given the difficulty of maintaining entangled states in large and complex systems.

The Role of Quantum Coherence

Another quantum phenomenon that may be relevant to the brain is quantum coherence. Coherence refers to the property of quantum systems in which the phases of different states are correlated. In a coherent system, the different states interfere with each other in a way that can lead to constructive or destructive interference.

One potential application of quantum coherence in the brain is in the processing of sensory information. It has been proposed that the brain may use quantum coherence to enhance the sensitivity of sensory systems to weak signals. In this model, the coherence of the states of neurons in sensory systems would allow for the amplification of weak signals, making them easier to detect.

However, the idea of quantum coherence playing a role in the brain remains controversial. While some studies have suggested that coherence may play a role in sensory processing, others have found little evidence to support this idea.

The Role of Quantum Computing

Finally, it is worth considering the potential role of quantum computing in the brain. Quantum computers are devices that use quantum mechanics to perform calculations that are difficult or impossible for classical computers. They do this by exploiting the quantum phenomena of superposition and entanglement to process information in parallel.

While quantum computers are still in the early stages of development, researchers have proposed that the brain may be using quantum computing to perform certain types of computations. One possibility is that quantum computing could be used to simulate the behavior of large and complex molecules, such as those involved in the sense of smell. These simulations would require a large number of calculations to be performed in parallel, which is precisely the type of task that quantum computers excel at.

Another potential application of quantum computing in the brain is in the processing of complex decision-making. It has been proposed that the brain may be using quantum computing to perform calculations that are beyond the capabilities of classical computers. For example, quantum computing could be used to simulate the behavior of networks of neurons, allowing the brain to make more accurate predictions about the outcome of decisions.

However, it is important to note that the idea of quantum computing playing a role in the brain is still highly speculative. While there is some evidence to suggest that quantum computing may be involved in certain types of neural computations, much more research is needed to fully understand the potential role of quantum computing in the brain.

Conclusion

In conclusion, quantum information processing is a rapidly developing field that is providing new insights into the workings of the brain. While the role of quantum mechanics in the brain is still highly speculative, there is growing evidence to suggest that it may play a crucial role in cognitive processes such as neural communication, sensory processing, and decision-making.

Understanding the role of quantum mechanics in the brain could have profound implications for our understanding of consciousness. By shedding light on the fundamental processes underlying neural computation, quantum information processing could help us to unravel the mysteries of how the brain creates our subjective experience of the world.

However, it is important to note that the field of quantum information processing in the brain is still in its infancy, and much more research is needed to fully understand the potential implications of quantum mechanics for cognitive processes. Nonetheless, the insights gained from this research could pave the way for new advances in neuroscience, and ultimately lead to a deeper understanding of the nature of consciousness itself.

CHAPTER 10.2: EXPERIMENTAL EVIDENCE FOR QUANTUM INFORMATION PROCESSING IN THE BRAIN

In recent years, researchers have been exploring the possibility that quantum mechanics plays a role in neural function and consciousness. While the idea of quantum information processing in the brain is still largely theoretical, there have been a number of studies that provide evidence to support the hypothesis.

Here are some examples of experimental evidence for quantum information processing in the brain:

1. Quantum tunneling in enzymes: One of the key processes in enzyme function is the ability to catalyze chemical reactions by reducing the activation energy required. This process is often accomplished through the use of quantum tunneling, in which a particle is able to cross a potential energy barrier without having enough energy to surmount it. In recent years, researchers have discovered evidence of quantum tunneling in several key enzymes involved in metabolic processes in the brain, suggesting that quantum mechanics may play a role in these processes.

For example, researchers at University College

London have shown that the enzyme adenosine triphosphate (ATP) synthase, which is involved in energy production in cells, uses quantum tunneling to help facilitate the movement of protons through its structure. This allows the enzyme to function more efficiently and could potentially explain the high energy efficiency of the brain.

2. Entanglement in photosynthesis: Photosynthesis is a complex process that involves the conversion of sunlight into chemical energy. In order to efficiently capture and utilize this energy, photosynthetic organisms have evolved a complex system of pigment molecules that can absorb photons and transfer their energy to other molecules. Recent studies have suggested that the process of energy transfer in photosynthesis may be facilitated by the phenomenon of quantum entanglement, in which two particles become correlated in a way that cannot be explained by classical physics.

    Researchers at the University of California, Berkeley have shown that the efficiency of energy transfer in photosynthesis is enhanced by the presence of quantum coherence and entanglement. They used a combination of experimental and theoretical methods to show that the energy transfer process is optimized to take advantage of these quantum effects. This suggests that quantum mechanics may play a crucial role in the function of photosynthesis in the brain, which is known to be highly energy-intensive.

3. Quantum coherence in microtubules: Microtubules are long, thin tubes that are an important component of the cytoskeleton in neurons. They

are also believed to play a role in transporting molecules and other structures within the cell. Some researchers have proposed that microtubules may be able to maintain quantum coherence, a property that allows particles to exist in multiple states at the same time, and that this coherence could play a role in neural function.

> Researchers at the University of Arizona have shown that microtubules are indeed capable of maintaining quantum coherence for relatively long periods of time, up to several microseconds. They used a combination of experimental and theoretical methods to show that the structure of microtubules is consistent with the requirements for quantum coherence, and that this coherence may play a role in neural function.

4. Quantum effects in sensory processing: Some researchers have suggested that quantum mechanics may play a role in sensory processing, particularly in the sense of smell. The process of olfaction involves the binding of odorant molecules to receptors in the nose, and it is unclear how the brain is able to differentiate between similar molecules. One hypothesis is that quantum coherence may allow for more precise discrimination between similar molecules.

> Researchers at the University of Tokyo have shown that quantum coherence can indeed enhance the ability of olfactory receptors to discriminate between similar odorant molecules. They used a combination of experimental and theoretical methods to show that quantum coherence can improve the selectivity of the receptors, potentially explaining how the brain is able to distinguish

between thousands of different odorant molecules.

While these studies provide intriguing evidence for the potential role of quantum mechanics in the brain, it is important to note that the evidence is still preliminary and subject to further investigation and replication.

One of the main challenges in studying quantum information processing in the brain is the difficulty of measuring and observing quantum phenomena at the neural level. Most experiments are conducted at the macroscopic level, and it is challenging to isolate and measure the specific quantum processes that may be occurring in the brain. In addition, the brain is a complex system with numerous interactions and feedback loops, making it difficult to determine causality between specific neural processes and quantum phenomena.

Another challenge is distinguishing between genuine quantum effects and classical phenomena that may give the appearance of quantum behavior. For example, some researchers have suggested that classical chaotic dynamics in the brain could give rise to behavior that resembles quantum phenomena. It is therefore crucial to design experiments that can distinguish between genuine quantum effects and classical behavior.

Despite these challenges, there is growing interest in investigating the potential role of quantum information processing in the brain. Future studies may utilize more advanced technologies such as quantum sensors and qubits to measure and manipulate quantum phenomena at the neural level. New experimental designs may also be developed to more effectively distinguish between genuine quantum effects and classical behavior.

Conclusion

The study of quantum information processing in the brain is a fascinating and rapidly evolving field that has the potential to shed new light on the nature of consciousness and cognition.

While the evidence for quantum phenomena in the brain is still preliminary, recent experimental studies have provided intriguing support for the idea that the brain may utilize quantum information processing to perform certain cognitive functions.

Further research is needed to better understand the specific quantum processes that may be occurring in the brain, and to determine the extent to which these processes contribute to cognitive function and consciousness. Advances in technology and experimental design may help to overcome some of the challenges in studying quantum information processing in the brain and pave the way for new insights into the mysteries of the mind.

CHAPTER 10.3: THE IMPLICATIONS OF QUANTUM INFORMATION PROCESSING FOR CONSCIOUSNESS

The implications of quantum information processing in the brain for consciousness are profound and far-reaching. If the brain does indeed utilize quantum information processing, it would challenge traditional views of consciousness as a purely classical phenomenon and could offer new insights into the nature of subjective experience.

One of the key implications of quantum information processing in the brain is the potential for non-locality. In quantum mechanics, non-locality refers to the phenomenon whereby two entangled particles can instantaneously affect each other's properties, regardless of the distance between them. If the brain utilizes entangled particles or other forms of quantum coherence, it could potentially allow for non-local communication between different regions of the brain.

This could have implications for the way we think about the unity of consciousness. Traditionally, consciousness has been viewed as a unified phenomenon that arises from the activity of the brain as a whole. However, if quantum coherence is involved in consciousness, it could mean that consciousness is not a purely local phenomenon but rather arises from the coordinated activity of entangled particles across different regions of the brain. This could challenge traditional views of the relationship between the brain and consciousness.

Another potential implication of quantum information processing in the brain is the potential for superposition and entanglement to contribute to subjective experience. In the Copenhagen interpretation of quantum mechanics, superposition refers to the idea that a particle can exist in multiple states simultaneously until it is observed or measured. If the brain utilizes superposition, it could potentially allow for the representation of multiple possibilities or perspectives in a single neural state.

Entanglement, on the other hand, could potentially allow for the integration of information across different modalities or perspectives. This could contribute to the unity of consciousness and the ability to integrate sensory information from different sources into a single coherent experience.

The potential role of quantum information processing in subjective experience raises interesting questions about the relationship between the physical processes in the brain and the subjective experience of consciousness. While we may be able to map neural activity to different aspects of subjective experience, it is still unclear how subjective experience arises from physical processes in the brain.

Theories such as integrated information theory (IIT) propose that consciousness arises from the integrated information generated by the brain, rather than from specific neural processes or structures. If the brain utilizes quantum information processing, it could potentially contribute to the integrated information generated by the brain and provide a new perspective on the relationship between the physical processes in the brain and subjective experience.

The potential implications of quantum information processing in the brain for consciousness are still largely speculative, and much more research is needed to better understand the specific mechanisms involved. However, the field of quantum consciousness offers a promising avenue for exploring the nature of subjective experience and the relationship between the brain and consciousness.

Conclusion

The study of quantum information processing in the brain is a rapidly evolving field that has the potential to offer new insights into the nature of consciousness and cognition. If the brain does indeed utilize quantum information processing, it could challenge traditional views of consciousness as a purely classical phenomenon and offer new perspectives on the relationship between the brain and subjective experience.

The implications of quantum information processing for consciousness are still largely speculative, and much more research is needed to better understand the specific mechanisms involved. However, recent experimental studies have provided intriguing evidence for the potential role of quantum coherence in the brain, and the field of quantum consciousness offers a promising avenue for exploring the mysteries of the mind.

CHAPTER 11: QUANTUM FIELD THEORY AND CONSCIOUSNESS

Quantum Field Theory (QFT) is a branch of physics that provides a theoretical framework for the study of the behavior of subatomic particles. It is the most accurate theory that we have to describe the behavior of matter and energy at the most fundamental level. However, QFT has also been applied to the study of consciousness, leading to the development of the theory of quantum consciousness. In this chapter, we will explore the relationship between QFT and consciousness, and how this relationship has been used to explain various aspects of human consciousness.

Quantum Field Theory

In QFT, particles are described as excitations of quantum fields, which permeate all of space. These fields are considered to be the fundamental entities of nature, and particles are simply localized disturbances in these fields. In other words, particles are not considered to be separate entities that exist independently of their environment. Instead, they are considered to be inseparable from the fields in which they exist. This idea is known as the wave-particle duality of quantum mechanics, which states that particles can behave like waves and waves can behave like particles.

The concept of a quantum field is one of the most important and counterintuitive concepts in modern physics. According to QFT, everything that we see around us is made up of quantum fields. These fields are in a constant state of flux, with particles appearing and disappearing spontaneously. This phenomenon is known as quantum fluctuation, and it is a consequence of Heisenberg's uncertainty principle, which states that the more precisely we measure the position of a particle, the less precisely we can measure its momentum, and vice versa.

The concept of quantum fields also has important implications for the study of consciousness. According to some theories of quantum consciousness, the brain can be thought of as a complex network of quantum fields, which interact with each other to produce the various aspects of human consciousness.

Quantum Consciousness

The theory of quantum consciousness is based on the idea that consciousness arises from the interaction of quantum fields in the brain. According to this theory, the brain is not a classical computer that processes information in a linear, step-by-step manner. Instead, it is a quantum computer that can process information in a parallel, non-linear manner. This means that the brain can perform multiple computations simultaneously, which allows it to process vast amounts of information in a short period of time.

The concept of quantum consciousness has been used to explain various aspects of human consciousness, such as the subjective experience of color, the sense of self, and the ability to make decisions. For example, the subjective experience of color is thought to arise from the interaction of quantum fields in the visual cortex. The sense of self is thought to arise from the interaction of quantum fields in the prefrontal cortex. And the ability to make decisions is thought to arise from the interaction of quantum fields in the striatum.

One of the most intriguing aspects of the theory of quantum consciousness is the idea that consciousness is not confined to the brain. According to this theory, consciousness is a fundamental aspect of the universe, and it permeates all of space. This idea is similar to the concept of the unified field in physics, which postulates that there is a single field that underlies all of the physical universe. In the theory of quantum consciousness, this unified field is thought to be the source of consciousness itself.

The concept of a unified field of consciousness has important implications for our understanding of the nature of reality. According to this theory, consciousness is not a byproduct of the physical universe, but rather a fundamental aspect of it. This means that consciousness and the physical universe are intimately connected, and that one cannot be understood without the other.

Critiques and Challenges

Despite the promise of the theory of quantum consciousness, it remains a highly controversial area of research. One of the main critiques of the theory is the lack of empirical evidence to support it. While there is some evidence to suggest that quantum mechanics may play a role in the brain, there is still a long way to go in terms of demonstrating a direct link between quantum fields and human consciousness.

Another challenge facing the theory of quantum consciousness is the difficulty in testing it. Unlike traditional scientific theories, which can be tested and validated through repeatable experiments, the theory of quantum consciousness is difficult to test because it deals with subjective experiences such as consciousness, which are difficult to measure objectively.

Moreover, there are also philosophical challenges to the theory of quantum consciousness. For example, some philosophers argue that consciousness cannot be reduced to the level of subatomic particles because it involves subjective experiences that cannot be explained solely in terms of physical processes.

Despite these challenges, the theory of quantum consciousness continues to generate interest and research in the scientific community. It offers a promising approach to understanding the complex phenomenon of human consciousness, and it may provide new insights into the nature of reality itself.

Conclusion

In conclusion, the relationship between Quantum Field Theory and consciousness is a complex and intriguing area of research. While the theory of quantum consciousness remains controversial, it offers a promising approach to understanding the nature of human consciousness and its relationship to the physical universe. The idea that consciousness is not confined to the brain but is a fundamental aspect of the universe has profound implications for our understanding of the nature of reality. As research in this area continues, we may gain a deeper understanding of the nature of consciousness and its place in the universe.

CHAPTER 11.1: DEFINITION OF QUANTUM FIELD THEORY

Quantum Field Theory (QFT) is a theoretical framework used to describe the behavior of subatomic particles. In the early 20th century, physicists discovered that the classical laws of physics could not fully explain the behavior of subatomic particles, such as electrons and protons. This led to the development of quantum mechanics, a new set of physical laws that could accurately describe the behavior of these particles.

However, while quantum mechanics was successful in describing the behavior of individual particles, it did not provide a comprehensive picture of the behavior of multiple particles interacting with each other. This led to the development of QFT, which describes particles as excitations of quantum fields that permeate all of space.

In QFT, particles are not considered to be separate entities that exist independently of their environment. Instead, they are considered to be inseparable from the fields in which they exist. The behavior of particles is described by the interactions between these fields, which can be quantified using mathematical equations.

One of the key concepts of QFT is the idea of quantization, which refers to the process of turning a continuous field into a discrete set of particles. This process is necessary because quantum mechanics describes particles in terms of discrete energy levels, rather than continuous energy levels.

QFT has been incredibly successful in describing the behavior of subatomic particles, and it has been used to make predictions that have been verified by experiments. For example, the theory predicted the existence of the Higgs boson particle, which was later discovered by the Large Hadron Collider.

QFT also has important implications for our understanding of the nature of reality. According to QFT, everything that we see around us is made up of quantum fields. These fields are in a constant state of flux, with particles appearing and disappearing spontaneously. This phenomenon is known as quantum fluctuation, and it is a consequence of Heisenberg's uncertainty principle, which states that the more precisely we measure the position of a particle, the less precisely we can measure its momentum, and vice versa.

The concept of quantum fields also has important implications for the study of consciousness. According to some theories of quantum consciousness, the brain can be thought of as a complex network of quantum fields, which interact with each other to produce the various aspects of human consciousness.

One of the challenges of QFT is that it can be difficult to calculate the behavior of particles in certain situations, such as when they are interacting with each other. This has led to the development of new mathematical techniques, such as perturbation theory and renormalization, which allow physicists to make accurate predictions about the behavior of particles in complex situations.

In conclusion, Quantum Field Theory is a theoretical framework that describes the behavior of subatomic particles as excitations of quantum fields that permeate all of space. It has been incredibly successful in describing the behavior of particles and has important implications for our understanding of the nature of reality. In the context of the study of consciousness, QFT provides a promising approach to understanding the complex phenomenon of human consciousness and its relationship to the physical universe.

CHAPTER 11.2: THE ROLE OF QUANTUM FIELD THEORY IN CONSCIOUSNESS

One of the most intriguing and controversial areas of research in the field of consciousness studies is the role of Quantum Field Theory (QFT) in explaining the nature of human consciousness. According to some theories of quantum consciousness, the brain can be thought of as a complex network of quantum fields, which interact with each other to produce the various aspects of human consciousness.

One of the key proponents of the theory of quantum consciousness is Stuart Hameroff, a professor of anesthesiology and psychology at the University of Arizona. Hameroff's theory, known as orchestrated objective reduction (Orch-OR), proposes that the microtubules within neurons in the brain are the key to understanding the relationship between consciousness and quantum mechanics.

According to the Orch-OR theory, microtubules are cylindrical structures that act as molecular-scale computers within neurons. These microtubules are thought to be capable of performing complex computations, and they are also thought to be sensitive to quantum fluctuations.

Hameroff proposes that when a neuron fires, the information within the neuron is broadcast to the microtubules, which then collapse the quantum state of the information into a classical state. This process is known as objective reduction, and it is thought to be responsible for the subjective experience of consciousness.

The Orch-OR theory has been met with some skepticism in the scientific community, with some researchers questioning whether microtubules are actually capable of performing the types of computations proposed by Hameroff. However, the theory continues to generate interest and research in the field of consciousness studies.

Another theory of quantum consciousness, proposed by Roger Penrose and others, suggests that consciousness arises from the collective behavior of quantum fields within the brain. According to this theory, consciousness is not confined to the brain but is a fundamental aspect of the universe itself.

Penrose and others propose that consciousness arises from the collapse of quantum superpositions in the brain, which leads to a reduction in the amount of entropy in the system. This reduction in entropy is thought to be responsible for the subjective experience of consciousness.

The idea that consciousness is a fundamental aspect of the universe is not new. In fact, it has been proposed by many philosophers and spiritual traditions throughout history. However, the idea that consciousness is related to quantum mechanics is a relatively recent development, and it has yet to be fully validated by empirical research.

Despite the controversy surrounding the theory of quantum consciousness, there are some indications that quantum mechanics may play a role in the brain. For example, researchers have observed quantum entanglement, a phenomenon in which two particles become correlated in such a way that their properties become dependent on each other, in biological systems such as photosynthesis.

There is also evidence to suggest that the brain may be able to process information using quantum algorithms, which are thought to be more efficient than classical algorithms. For example, researchers have observed that the human eye is capable of detecting a single photon of light, which suggests that the brain is capable of processing information at the quantum level.

Despite these indications, however, there is still a long way to go in terms of demonstrating a direct link between quantum mechanics and human consciousness. One of the main challenges facing researchers in this area is the difficulty of testing the theory of quantum consciousness. Consciousness is a subjective experience, and it is difficult to measure objectively.

Another challenge is the lack of empirical evidence to support the theory. While there is some evidence to suggest that quantum mechanics may play a role in the brain, there is still much research to be done in order to fully understand the relationship between quantum mechanics and consciousness.

In conclusion, the role of Quantum Field Theory in consciousness is a complex and controversial area of research. While there are indications that quantum mechanics may play a role in the brain, the exact nature of this relationship is still unclear. The theory of quantum consciousness is just one of many theories attempting to explain the nature of human consciousness, and it is likely that it will continue to generate interest and debate in the scientific community for years to come.

It is important to note that the theory of quantum consciousness is still in its early stages of development, and much more research is needed to fully understand its potential implications. Nevertheless, the theory has already spurred important discussions about the nature of consciousness and the role of quantum mechanics in the brain.

One potential application of the theory of quantum consciousness is in the field of artificial intelligence. As researchers work to develop more advanced AI systems, understanding the relationship between consciousness and quantum mechanics may be crucial to creating machines that are truly intelligent and self-aware.

Overall, the role of Quantum Field Theory in consciousness is an exciting area of research that has the potential to transform our understanding of the human mind. While the theory of quantum consciousness is still in its infancy, it offers a fascinating glimpse into the intersection of quantum mechanics and consciousness, and it is likely to generate significant interest and research in the years to come.

CHAPTER 11.3: EXPERIMENTAL EVIDENCE FOR QUANTUM FIELD THEORY AND CONSCIOUSNESS

The theory of quantum consciousness suggests that the principles of quantum mechanics play a crucial role in the functioning of the human brain and the emergence of consciousness. However, as with any scientific theory, experimental evidence is needed to support these claims. In this section, we will explore some of the experimental evidence that has been put forth in support of the theory of quantum consciousness.

One of the most compelling pieces of evidence for the theory of quantum consciousness comes from experiments involving quantum entanglement. Quantum entanglement is a phenomenon in which two particles become connected in such a way that the state of one particle is dependent on the state of the other, regardless of the distance between them. In recent years, researchers have begun to explore the possibility that entanglement may be involved in the transmission of information within the brain.

One such experiment was conducted by a team of researchers led by Anirban Bandyopadhyay at the National Institute for Materials Science in Japan. The researchers observed a form of entanglement known as Bell-type non-locality in a sample of brain tissue from a rat. This suggests that entanglement may play a role in the transmission of information within the brain, potentially supporting the theory of quantum consciousness.

Another piece of experimental evidence comes from studies of quantum tunneling. Quantum tunneling is a phenomenon in which a particle is able to pass through a barrier that it would not normally be able to pass through, due to the probabilistic nature of quantum mechanics. This process is thought to occur within the brain, where it may play a role in synaptic transmission.

One study, conducted by Travis Craddock and colleagues at the University of New Mexico, used a technique known as transcranial magnetic stimulation to stimulate the brains of participants while they were undergoing functional magnetic resonance imaging (fMRI). The researchers found that the stimulation caused changes in the fMRI signal that were consistent with quantum tunneling. This provides some evidence for the idea that quantum mechanics may be involved in the functioning of the brain.

Other experiments have focused on the idea of quantum coherence, which refers to the ability of particles to maintain their quantum state over time. Researchers have suggested that quantum coherence may be involved in the synchronization of neuronal firing within the brain, which is thought to be important for the emergence of consciousness.

One study, conducted by Anil Seth and colleagues at the University of Sussex, used a technique known as magnetoencephalography to measure the magnetic fields produced by the brain. The researchers found evidence for long-range quantum coherence within the brain, which they suggested could be involved in the synchronization of neuronal firing.

While these experimental results are intriguing, it is important to note that they are still in the early stages of development. More research is needed to fully understand the role that quantum mechanics plays in the functioning of the brain, and how this relates to the emergence of consciousness.

There are also some challenges to the interpretation of these experimental results in terms of the theory of quantum consciousness. For example, some researchers have suggested that the observed quantum effects may be due to other factors, such as environmental noise or classical correlations between particles.

Additionally, some researchers have argued that the observed quantum effects are simply a consequence of the probabilistic nature of quantum mechanics, and do not necessarily imply a role for quantum mechanics in the functioning of the brain. These criticisms highlight the need for further research in this area, in order to fully understand the potential implications of the theory of quantum consciousness.

In conclusion, the experimental evidence for the theory of quantum consciousness is still in its early stages, but it is an exciting area of research that has the potential to transform our understanding of the human mind. The studies involving quantum entanglement, quantum tunneling, and quantum coherence provide intriguing support for the idea that quantum mechanics may play a role in the functioning of the brain and the emergence of consciousness. However, it is important to note that these experimental results are still subject to interpretation and further research is needed to fully understand their implications.

Moreover, it is important to note that even if the experimental evidence for the theory of quantum consciousness is confirmed, it would not necessarily mean that classical mechanics is completely irrelevant to the functioning of the brain. In fact, many scientists believe that a combination of quantum and classical mechanics is likely involved in the emergence of consciousness.

Furthermore, the theory of quantum consciousness has been met with skepticism by some scientists, who argue that the idea of quantum mechanics playing a role in consciousness is unfounded and that classical physics is sufficient to explain the emergence of consciousness. They argue that the complexity of the brain is already explained by classical physics, and there is no need to invoke quantum mechanics.

Despite these critiques, the theory of quantum consciousness continues to be an active area of research, with many scientists working to explore the potential implications of quantum mechanics for the functioning of the brain and the emergence of consciousness. As new experimental techniques and technologies are developed, it is likely that we will gain a deeper understanding of the relationship between quantum mechanics and consciousness.

In conclusion, the role of quantum field theory in consciousness is a complex and fascinating area of research. While there are indications that quantum mechanics may play a role in the functioning of the brain and the emergence of consciousness, there is still much to be learned. The experimental evidence for the theory of quantum consciousness is still in its early stages, and further research is needed to fully understand the implications of these findings. Regardless of the ultimate outcome of this research, the study of quantum consciousness has the potential to transform our understanding of the human mind and our place in the universe.

CHAPTER 12: QUANTUM MECHANICS AND THE NATURE OF REALITY

Quantum mechanics is a field of physics that studies the behavior of matter and energy at the atomic and subatomic level. It has been incredibly successful in explaining the behavior of particles at this scale, and its predictions have been confirmed through numerous experiments. However, the implications of quantum mechanics for our understanding of the nature of reality are profound and controversial. In this chapter, we will explore some of the key concepts in quantum mechanics and their implications for our understanding of reality.

The Uncertainty Principle

One of the key concepts in quantum mechanics is the uncertainty principle. This principle states that it is impossible to know the precise position and momentum of a particle at the same time. The more precisely we know one of these quantities, the less precisely we can know the other. This is not due to limitations in our technology or measurement techniques, but is a fundamental property of the universe.

The implications of the uncertainty principle are profound. It means that at the subatomic level, particles do not have a well-defined position or momentum. Instead, they exist in a state of probability, where the probability of finding a particle in a particular position or with a particular momentum can be calculated.

The Copenhagen Interpretation

The Copenhagen interpretation is one of the most widely accepted interpretations of quantum mechanics. It was developed by Niels Bohr and his colleagues in the 1920s and 1930s, and it holds that the behavior of particles at the subatomic level is inherently probabilistic. The Copenhagen interpretation also holds that particles do not have a definite existence until they are observed or measured.

This interpretation has been controversial, as it seems to imply that the act of observation or measurement can affect the behavior of particles. This has led some scientists and philosophers to question the idea that there is an objective reality that exists independently of observation.

Quantum Entanglement

Another key concept in quantum mechanics is quantum entanglement. This occurs when two particles become entangled, such that the state of one particle is linked to the state of the other. When two entangled particles are separated, the state of each particle remains linked to the other, regardless of the distance between them.

The implications of quantum entanglement are profound, as it seems to violate our traditional understanding of causality and locality. It implies that particles can be linked in ways that transcend the usual limits of space and time. This has led some scientists and philosophers to speculate that there may be a deeper, non-local reality that underlies the apparent separateness of the physical world.

The Many-Worlds Interpretation

The Many-Worlds interpretation is another controversial interpretation of quantum mechanics. It holds that every time a quantum measurement is made, the universe splits into multiple branches, each corresponding to a different outcome of the measurement. In this interpretation, all possible outcomes of a measurement exist in separate, parallel universes.

This interpretation has been criticized for its lack of empirical support, as it is difficult to imagine how we could ever test the idea of multiple parallel universes. However, it has also been praised for its ability to explain some of the strange and seemingly paradoxical aspects of quantum mechanics.

Implications for the Nature of Reality

The implications of quantum mechanics for our understanding of the nature of reality are profound and controversial. Some scientists and philosophers argue that quantum mechanics implies that there is no objective reality that exists independently of observation. They point to the fact that the act of measurement seems to affect the behavior of particles, and that particles do not have a well-defined existence until they are observed.

Others argue that quantum mechanics does not necessarily imply that there is no objective reality. They point out that even in the probabilistic world of quantum mechanics, there are still patterns and regularities that can be observed and studied. They suggest that these patterns may indicate the existence of a deeper underlying reality that we have yet to fully understand.

Another interpretation of quantum mechanics that supports the idea of an objective reality is the Many-Worlds Interpretation. According to this interpretation, every time a measurement is made, the universe splits into multiple branches, each representing a different outcome. In this way, all possible outcomes of a measurement exist simultaneously in different branches of the universe. While this interpretation is controversial and has its own set of challenges, it does suggest that there may be an objective reality that exists independently of our observations.

Overall, the debate about the nature of reality in quantum mechanics is ongoing and complex. While some argue that it implies the non-existence of objective reality, others suggest that there may be a deeper underlying reality that we have yet to fully understand. Nevertheless, the discoveries made in quantum mechanics have challenged our traditional understanding of the universe and continue to spark new avenues of research and exploration.

Quantum Mechanics and Consciousness

The discoveries made in quantum mechanics have also led to speculation about the role of quantum mechanics in consciousness. Some researchers have suggested that the strange and seemingly inexplicable behavior of subatomic particles may provide clues about the nature of consciousness.

One theory that has been proposed is the Orch-OR theory, which suggests that consciousness arises from quantum events that occur in microtubules inside neurons. According to this theory, the quantum events cause the microtubules to collapse into a single coherent state, leading to the emergence of conscious experience.

However, the Orch-OR theory is controversial and has been widely criticized by other researchers. Some argue that the theory is too speculative and lacks empirical evidence to support it. Others suggest that the idea of quantum events influencing consciousness is unlikely, given that the brain is a warm, wet, and noisy environment, which is not conducive to maintaining quantum coherence.

Despite the challenges and controversies surrounding the Orch-OR theory, the idea that quantum mechanics may play a role in consciousness continues to attract interest from researchers. Some have suggested that the non-locality and entanglement observed in quantum mechanics may provide a mechanism for the unity of consciousness. Others have suggested that the probabilistic nature of quantum mechanics may provide a way to account for the free will that we experience.

Conclusion

Quantum mechanics has challenged our traditional understanding of the universe and continues to spark new avenues of research and exploration. While the discoveries made in quantum mechanics have led to speculation about the nature of reality and consciousness, the debate about these topics is ongoing and complex.

While some argue that quantum mechanics implies the non-existence of objective reality, others suggest that there may be a deeper underlying reality that we have yet to fully understand. Similarly, the idea that quantum mechanics may play a role in consciousness remains controversial and lacks empirical evidence to support it.

Nevertheless, the discoveries made in quantum mechanics have opened up new possibilities for understanding the universe and our place within it. The exploration of these possibilities is a crucial area of research that has the potential to transform our understanding of the human mind and our place in the cosmos.

CHAPTER 12.1: THE COPENHAGEN INTERPRETATION OF QUANTUM MECHANICS

Quantum mechanics is a fundamental theory of physics that describes the behavior of subatomic particles. It was developed in the early 20th century and has since revolutionized our understanding of the universe. However, quantum mechanics has also sparked intense debate and speculation about the nature of reality, consciousness, and the universe itself.

One of the most influential interpretations of quantum mechanics is the Copenhagen interpretation. This interpretation was developed by a group of physicists, including Niels Bohr, Werner Heisenberg, and Max Born, in the 1920s and 1930s. The Copenhagen interpretation is based on the idea that the act of measurement plays a fundamental role in quantum mechanics.

According to the Copenhagen interpretation, subatomic particles do not have definite properties, such as position or momentum, until they are observed or measured. Prior to measurement, subatomic particles exist in a state of superposition, meaning that they exist in all possible states simultaneously. However, when a measurement is made, the superposition collapses, and the particle is found in one definite state.

The act of measurement is central to the Copenhagen

interpretation because it is believed to play a fundamental role in determining the properties of subatomic particles. In other words, the outcome of a measurement is not determined by the properties of the particle itself, but rather by the act of measurement.

The Copenhagen interpretation has been incredibly influential in the development of quantum mechanics and has been used to explain many phenomena observed in the subatomic world. However, it has also sparked intense debate and speculation about the nature of reality and the role of consciousness in the universe.

Critiques of the Copenhagen Interpretation

One of the main critiques of the Copenhagen interpretation is that it implies that there is no objective reality. If the properties of subatomic particles are determined by the act of measurement, then it suggests that there is no underlying reality that exists independently of our observations.

This idea has been widely debated among physicists and philosophers, with some arguing that it implies a form of subjective idealism, where reality is created by our observations. Others argue that quantum mechanics does not necessarily imply that there is no objective reality. They point out that even in the probabilistic world of quantum mechanics, there are still patterns and regularities that can be observed and studied. They suggest that these patterns may indicate the existence of a deeper underlying reality that we have yet to fully understand.

Another critique of the Copenhagen interpretation is that it is incomplete. The interpretation does not provide a clear explanation of how the collapse of the wave function occurs or what determines the outcome of a measurement. This has led to the development of alternative interpretations, such as the Many-Worlds Interpretation and the Bohmian Interpretation, which seek to provide a more complete and deterministic explanation of quantum mechanics.

The Copenhagen Interpretation and Consciousness

The Copenhagen interpretation has also been linked to the role of consciousness in the universe. Some researchers have suggested that the act of measurement in quantum mechanics is analogous to the act of observation in consciousness.

According to this view, just as subatomic particles do not have definite properties until they are observed, consciousness also creates reality through observation. In other words, the act of observation by a conscious observer is what collapses the wave function and determines the properties of the subatomic particle.

However, this view has been widely criticized by other researchers, who argue that it is too speculative and lacks empirical evidence. They suggest that the relationship between quantum mechanics and consciousness is still poorly understood and requires further research and investigation.

Conclusion

The Copenhagen interpretation of quantum mechanics has been incredibly influential in the development of quantum mechanics and our understanding of the subatomic world. It is based on the idea that the act of measurement plays a fundamental role in determining the properties of subatomic particles.

However, the Copenhagen interpretation has faced criticism and challenges from other interpretations of quantum mechanics. Some critics argue that it leads to a subjectivist and even solipsistic view of reality, where the observer is the ultimate determinant of what exists and what doesn't.

Moreover, the Copenhagen interpretation is inherently limited in its ability to provide a complete picture of the nature of reality. It is focused on the behavior of subatomic particles and does not offer insights into the behavior of larger objects or complex systems, such as the human brain.

Nonetheless, the Copenhagen interpretation has been immensely influential and has led to many important developments in quantum mechanics. It has inspired new ways of thinking about the nature of reality, the role of observation in scientific inquiry, and the limits of our knowledge.

As our understanding of quantum mechanics continues to evolve, it is likely that new interpretations and theories will emerge. The Copenhagen interpretation will likely remain an important part of the conversation, but it is important to remain open to new ideas and perspectives that may help us gain a deeper understanding of the universe we inhabit.

CHAPTER 12.2: THE MANY-WORLDS INTERPRETATION OF QUANTUM MECHANICS

The Many-Worlds Interpretation of quantum mechanics is a fascinating theory that has been proposed as an alternative to the Copenhagen Interpretation. It was first introduced by Hugh Everett in 1957, and it has gained a growing following in recent years. This interpretation suggests that instead of collapsing into a single outcome as the Copenhagen Interpretation suggests, the wave function of a quantum system never truly collapses, but rather it branches off into multiple parallel universes, each one representing a different outcome of the quantum measurement.

According to the Many-Worlds Interpretation, every possible outcome of a quantum measurement actually occurs, but each one exists in a separate parallel universe. For example, if a quantum particle is in a superposition of two states, then according to this interpretation, there are actually two separate universes in which the particle is in each of those states. This idea has been popularized in science fiction, where it is sometimes referred to as the "multiverse" theory.

One of the main strengths of the Many-Worlds Interpretation is that it avoids some of the paradoxes and difficulties that arise in the Copenhagen Interpretation. For example, in the Copenhagen Interpretation, the wave function collapses randomly into one of the possible outcomes, which raises questions about why certain outcomes occur and others do not. The Many-Worlds Interpretation offers a more elegant solution to this problem, suggesting that all possible outcomes actually occur in separate parallel universes.

Furthermore, the Many-Worlds Interpretation also offers a way to reconcile the probabilistic nature of quantum mechanics with the determinism of classical mechanics. In classical mechanics, the behavior of particles can be predicted with certainty based on their initial conditions. However, in quantum mechanics, the behavior of particles is described by probabilities. The Many-Worlds Interpretation suggests that while the probabilities in each universe are still uncertain, the overall outcome across all parallel universes is deterministic.

Critics of the Many-Worlds Interpretation have argued that the theory is speculative and unfalsifiable. Since we cannot observe the other parallel universes directly, there is no way to test the theory empirically. Additionally, some critics argue that the Many-Worlds Interpretation raises more questions than it answers, such as the question of what defines a "branching event" in the universe and why certain outcomes occur more frequently than others.

Despite these criticisms, the Many-Worlds Interpretation remains an intriguing and thought-provoking theory in the realm of quantum mechanics. It challenges our understanding of the nature of reality and raises important philosophical questions about the nature of the universe and our place within it.

Moreover, the Many-Worlds Interpretation has implications beyond the realm of quantum mechanics. It has been suggested that the theory could provide a solution to the problem of consciousness, by suggesting that consciousness arises from the interaction between multiple parallel universes. This idea has been explored in depth by some proponents of the theory, who argue that consciousness is an emergent property of the vast network of parallel universes that make up the multiverse.

In conclusion, the Many-Worlds Interpretation of quantum

mechanics is a fascinating theory that challenges our understanding of the nature of reality. While it remains controversial and unproven, it offers a compelling alternative to the Copenhagen Interpretation and has inspired new ways of thinking about the universe and our place within it. As our understanding of quantum mechanics continues to evolve, it is likely that new interpretations and theories will emerge, and the Many-Worlds Interpretation will continue to be an important part of the conversation.

CHAPTER 12.3: IMPLICATIONS OF QUANTUM MECHANICS FOR THE NATURE OF REALITY AND CONSCIOUSNESS

Quantum mechanics has revolutionized our understanding of the subatomic world, but it has also raised deep and challenging questions about the nature of reality and consciousness. In this chapter, we will explore some of the implications of quantum mechanics for these fundamental questions.

First, let's review the basic tenets of quantum mechanics. As we discussed earlier, quantum mechanics is based on the principle of superposition, which allows subatomic particles to exist in multiple states simultaneously. However, when a measurement is made, the wave function collapses and the particle is observed to be in a definite state.

This principle has led to two major interpretations of quantum mechanics: the Copenhagen interpretation and the many-worlds interpretation. The Copenhagen interpretation, as we discussed in the previous section, asserts that the act of measurement plays a fundamental role in determining the properties of subatomic particles. The many-worlds interpretation, on the other hand, proposes that every possible outcome of a quantum event actually occurs in a separate universe, resulting in a branching of the universe into multiple parallel realities.

So, what do these interpretations mean for the nature of reality and consciousness? Let's explore some of the implications.

1. Reality is probabilistic and observer-dependent
   One of the most striking implications of quantum mechanics is that the properties of subatomic particles are not determined until they are observed. This means that reality is probabilistic rather than deterministic, and that the act of observation plays a fundamental role in shaping reality.

   This has led some philosophers and scientists to question the notion of objective reality. If the properties of particles are observer-dependent, then how can we say that there is a single objective reality that exists independently of observation? Some have argued that this implies a form of subjective idealism, where the mind plays a fundamental role in creating reality.

2. Consciousness and the measurement problem
   The measurement problem in quantum mechanics refers to the fact that the act of measurement collapses the wave function and determines the properties of subatomic particles. This raises the question of how consciousness is involved in the measurement process.

   Some have proposed that consciousness plays a fundamental role in the measurement process, either as the observer who collapses the wave function or as the agent that selects the specific outcome of a quantum event. This has led to the theory of quantum consciousness, which proposes that consciousness is a fundamental aspect of the universe and that it plays a crucial role in the behavior of subatomic particles.

However, this theory remains controversial and has been subject to criticism. Some argue that there is no evidence to support the notion that consciousness plays a causal role in quantum events, and that the theory of quantum consciousness is based on a misunderstanding of quantum mechanics.

3. The many-worlds interpretation and the nature of consciousness

    The many-worlds interpretation proposes that every possible outcome of a quantum event actually occurs in a separate universe, resulting in a branching of the universe into multiple parallel realities. This implies that there are an infinite number of parallel versions of ourselves, each experiencing a different outcome of a quantum event.

    This has led some to question the nature of consciousness and personal identity. If there are multiple versions of ourselves, which version is the "real" one? How can we say that we are a single, continuous self when there are infinite versions of ourselves existing in parallel universes?

4. Implications for free will

    Finally, quantum mechanics has implications for the concept of free will. If the behavior of subatomic particles is probabilistic and observer-dependent, then how can we say that we have free will? Some argue that the randomness inherent in quantum mechanics provides a basis for free will, while others argue that it undermines the concept of free will altogether.

Conclusion

Quantum mechanics has challenged our fundamental assumptions about the nature of reality and has raised deep philosophical questions about the relationship between consciousness and the physical world. While the Copenhagen interpretation and the Many-Worlds interpretation offer different perspectives on the nature of reality, both acknowledge the bizarre and counterintuitive nature of quantum mechanics.

The implications of quantum mechanics for consciousness are particularly intriguing. The idea that consciousness may play a role in the act of measurement and collapse of the wave function is a radical departure from traditional views of the relationship between the observer and the observed.

The possibility that consciousness is an inherent part of the fabric of the universe has far-reaching implications for our understanding of ourselves and the world around us. It suggests that the human mind may have a profound influence on the physical world, and that our perception of reality may be shaped by the very act of observation.

However, the precise nature of this relationship between consciousness and quantum mechanics remains elusive. While some theories, such as the Orch-OR theory, propose a specific mechanism for this interaction, others remain speculative.

Ultimately, the nature of reality and consciousness remains one of the greatest mysteries of the universe. The study of quantum mechanics has given us new insights into the fundamental nature of the universe, but it has also raised new questions that challenge our existing beliefs and assumptions.

As we continue to explore the mysteries of the quantum world, it is likely that our understanding of the nature of reality and consciousness will continue to evolve. The study of quantum consciousness offers a promising avenue for exploring these questions and unlocking the secrets of the universe.

CHAPTER 13: QUANTUM CONSCIOUSNESS AND MYSTICISM

The intersection between quantum mechanics and mysticism has been a subject of fascination for many years. Both quantum mechanics and mysticism challenge our traditional views of the nature of reality, and there is a growing body of research that suggests that these two seemingly disparate fields may be more closely related than we previously thought.

In this chapter, we will explore the connections between quantum mechanics and mysticism, and how these connections may shed light on the nature of consciousness.

Quantum Mechanics and Mysticism

One of the most striking similarities between quantum mechanics and mysticism is the idea that reality is not fixed and objective, but rather subjective and dependent on the observer. In quantum mechanics, the act of observation plays a fundamental role in determining the properties of subatomic particles. Similarly, in many mystical traditions, the individual's perception and consciousness shape their reality.

Another similarity is the idea that reality is interconnected and that everything is part of a larger whole. In quantum mechanics, entanglement suggests that particles can be linked in ways that transcend space and time, while in mysticism, there is the concept of unity consciousness, in which the individual realizes their interconnectedness with all things.

Additionally, both quantum mechanics and mysticism challenge our traditional notions of causality. In quantum mechanics, the probabilistic nature of subatomic particles means that events can occur without a clear cause-and-effect relationship. Similarly, in mysticism, there is the concept of synchronicity, in which seemingly unrelated events are connected in a meaningful way.

The Role of Mysticism in Understanding Consciousness

Mysticism offers a unique perspective on consciousness that complements the insights provided by quantum mechanics. While quantum mechanics offers a scientific framework for understanding the physical world, mysticism offers a more subjective and experiential understanding of the nature of consciousness.

Mystical experiences, such as those reported by meditators and contemplatives, are characterized by a sense of unity consciousness and transcendence of the ego. These experiences suggest that there may be a fundamental unity underlying all of reality, and that our sense of self may be an illusion.

This view is supported by some interpretations of quantum mechanics, such as the Many-Worlds interpretation, which suggests that all possible outcomes of an event actually occur in parallel universes. This view challenges the traditional notion of a fixed and objective reality, and suggests that our perception of reality may be shaped by our consciousness.

The Potential for Quantum Mysticism

The study of quantum consciousness and mysticism has the potential to transform our understanding of the nature of consciousness and the universe as a whole. By bringing together the insights of quantum mechanics and mysticism, we may be able to develop a more comprehensive understanding of the nature of reality and the role of consciousness within it.

One potential avenue for exploring this connection is through the use of entheogens, such as psilocybin and DMT, which have been used for centuries in mystical and shamanic practices. These substances have been shown to induce mystical experiences and alter consciousness in ways that may be related to the insights of quantum mechanics.

Another potential avenue is through the study of consciousness in the context of non-dualistic philosophies, such as Advaita Vedanta and Buddhism. These philosophies emphasize the non-dual nature of reality and the interconnectedness of all things, and may provide a framework for understanding the relationship between consciousness and quantum mechanics.

Critiques and Challenges

As with any area of research that challenges traditional views, the study of quantum consciousness and mysticism has faced its share of critiques and challenges. Some critics argue that the connections between quantum mechanics and mysticism are based on superficial similarities rather than any deeper connections.

Additionally, the use of entheogens in exploring these connections is controversial, and their effects on consciousness are not fully understood. Some argue that the experiences induced by these substances are not truly mystical, but rather chemical alterations of brain activity.

Furthermore, the idea that quantum mechanics can explain mystical experiences is still highly speculative and lacks rigorous empirical evidence. Some researchers argue that the subjective nature of mystical experiences makes it difficult to study them in a scientific manner, and that the use of quantum mechanics as an explanation is premature.

Despite these challenges, the exploration of the connections between quantum mechanics and mysticism remains an active area of research, and it is clear that the insights gained from both fields can inform and enrich one another.

Conclusion

The study of quantum consciousness and mysticism represents a fascinating intersection of two seemingly disparate fields of inquiry. While the connections between quantum mechanics and mysticism are still largely speculative, they offer a tantalizing possibility of a deeper understanding of the nature of consciousness and the universe.

Through the exploration of entheogenic experiences, mystical traditions, and the theories of quantum mechanics, researchers are beginning to unravel the mysteries of the mind and the cosmos. The insights gained from these investigations may have profound implications for our understanding of the nature of reality and our place in it.

While there is still much to learn and explore, the study of quantum consciousness and mysticism represents a bold and exciting direction in the search for greater knowledge and understanding of ourselves and the world around us.

CHAPTER 13.1: THE CONNECTION BETWEEN QUANTUM CONSCIOUSNESS AND MYSTICISM

The connection between quantum mechanics and mysticism is a topic that has fascinated many researchers and philosophers for decades. There are several intriguing similarities between the two fields, including the notion of interconnectedness, the role of consciousness in shaping reality, and the concept of non-duality. In this chapter, we will explore the connections between quantum consciousness and mysticism in more detail.

Interconnectedness

One of the central concepts in both quantum mechanics and mysticism is the idea of interconnectedness. In quantum mechanics, this is demonstrated through the phenomenon of entanglement, which describes how two particles can become connected in such a way that the state of one particle is dependent on the state of the other particle, regardless of the distance between them. This suggests that there is a fundamental interconnectedness between all things in the universe, which is not limited by space or time.

Similarly, in many spiritual and mystical traditions, there is a belief in the interconnectedness of all things. This is often expressed through concepts such as oneness, unity, or interbeing. The idea is that all things in the universe are fundamentally interconnected and interdependent, and that we are all part of a larger whole. This notion of interconnectedness suggests that our actions and thoughts can have a ripple effect on the world around us, and that we are all responsible for creating a better world.

The Role of Consciousness

Another area where quantum mechanics and mysticism intersect is in the role of consciousness in shaping reality. In quantum mechanics, the act of measurement is said to collapse the wave function, which determines the state of a particle. This implies that the observer plays an active role in determining the outcome of an experiment.

Similarly, in many spiritual and mystical traditions, there is a belief that our consciousness plays a fundamental role in shaping our reality. This is often expressed through concepts such as the power of positive thinking, visualization, and meditation. The idea is that our thoughts and intentions can influence the world around us, and that we have the ability to create our own reality through our consciousness.

Non-Duality

Finally, both quantum mechanics and mysticism point to the concept of non-duality. In quantum mechanics, the wave-particle duality suggests that particles can exhibit both wave-like and particle-like behavior, depending on the context of the experiment. This implies that the nature of reality is not fixed or static, but rather depends on the observer's perspective.

Similarly, in many spiritual and mystical traditions, there is a belief in the concept of non-duality, which suggests that there is no separation between the self and the universe. This is often expressed through concepts such as oneness, unity, and nondual awareness. The idea is that our sense of separation and individuality is an illusion, and that we are all interconnected and part of a larger whole.

Critiques and Challenges

As with any area of research that challenges traditional views, the study of quantum consciousness and mysticism has faced its share of critiques and challenges. Some critics argue that the connections between quantum mechanics and mysticism are based on superficial similarities rather than any deeper connections.

For example, physicist Sean Carroll has argued that the connections between quantum mechanics and consciousness are often overstated, and that there is no evidence to suggest that consciousness plays a fundamental role in quantum mechanics. Similarly, philosopher Massimo Pigliucci has criticized the use of mystical concepts in scientific discourse, arguing that they are not well-defined and can lead to confusion and misunderstandings.

Additionally, the use of entheogens in exploring these connections is controversial, and their effects on consciousness are not fully understood. While some researchers argue that entheogens can provide insights into the nature of consciousness and the universe, others caution that they can also lead to delusions and harmful experiences.

Despite these challenges and critiques, the connection between quantum consciousness and mysticism continues to be explored by researchers in the field. By examining the similarities between the two, they hope to gain a deeper understanding of the nature of consciousness and reality.

One area of overlap between quantum consciousness and mysticism is the concept of non-dualism. Non-dualism is the idea that there is no separation between the self and the universe, and that everything is interconnected. This is similar to the quantum mechanical concept of entanglement, which describes how particles can be connected in a way that their states are linked, regardless of the distance between them.

Many mystics have described experiencing a state of oneness or unity with the universe, which is similar to the state of entanglement. Some researchers argue that this connection between non-dualism and entanglement suggests that the experience of unity is not simply a subjective feeling, but rather a fundamental aspect of reality.

Another area of overlap between quantum consciousness and mysticism is the concept of the observer effect. In quantum mechanics, the act of observation can change the behavior of subatomic particles. Similarly, many mystical traditions emphasize the role of consciousness in shaping the nature of reality.

Some researchers suggest that the observer effect could be a manifestation of the idea that consciousness plays a fundamental role in creating reality. This is consistent with the idea that the universe is a holistic entity, in which the observer is not separate from the observed.

Additionally, some mystics have described experiencing a state of heightened consciousness or expanded awareness, which is similar to the quantum mechanical concept of superposition. In superposition, a particle can exist in multiple states at once, until it is observed and collapses into a single state. Similarly, some researchers suggest that the experience of expanded awareness may be a manifestation of the ability of consciousness to exist in multiple states simultaneously.

Critics of the connection between quantum consciousness and mysticism argue that the similarities between the two are superficial and do not indicate any deeper connections. However, proponents of the theory argue that these similarities are not mere coincidences, but rather indications of a fundamental unity between consciousness and the universe.

In conclusion, the connection between quantum consciousness and mysticism is a fascinating area of research that has the potential to deepen our understanding of the nature of consciousness and reality. By exploring the similarities between the two, researchers hope to gain insights into the fundamental nature of the universe and our place within it.

While there are challenges and critiques of this connection, the overlap between non-dualism and entanglement, the observer effect, and superposition provide compelling evidence that there may be deeper connections between these two seemingly disparate fields. As research in this area continues, we may come to a greater understanding of the fundamental nature of reality, and our place within it.

CHAPTER 13.2: THE IMPLICATIONS OF QUANTUM CONSCIOUSNESS FOR SPIRITUALITY

The study of quantum consciousness has implications for spirituality and the way we understand our relationship with the universe. In this chapter, we will explore some of these implications and how they relate to various spiritual beliefs.

One of the key implications of quantum consciousness is the idea of non-duality. Non-duality is a spiritual concept that suggests that everything is connected and ultimately one. In the context of quantum mechanics, this idea is supported by the concept of entanglement, which suggests that particles can be linked in such a way that their properties are interdependent regardless of distance.

This idea of non-duality is found in many spiritual traditions, including Hinduism, Buddhism, and Taoism. In Hinduism, it is represented by the concept of Advaita, which suggests that there is no distinction between the individual self and the ultimate reality. Similarly, in Buddhism, the concept of Sunyata suggests that all phenomena are ultimately empty and interconnected.

Quantum mechanics also challenges our traditional understanding of cause and effect. In classical mechanics, cause and effect are seen as separate entities, with cause preceding effect. However, in the probabilistic world of quantum mechanics, there is no clear distinction between cause and effect. This challenges our understanding of free will and the idea that our choices are predetermined.

This idea has implications for spirituality and the concept of karma. In Hinduism, Buddhism, and Jainism, karma refers to the idea that our actions have consequences that determine our future experiences. However, if cause and effect are not distinct entities, then it is difficult to argue that our actions have a predetermined outcome.

This leads to the concept of quantum karma, which suggests that our choices have an effect on the probabilistic outcomes of the universe. In other words, our choices can influence the way the universe unfolds, even though the ultimate outcome is uncertain.

Another implication of quantum consciousness for spirituality is the idea of interconnectedness. In the probabilistic world of quantum mechanics, particles are not isolated entities, but rather are connected to each other in a web of relationships. This suggests that everything in the universe is interconnected in some way, and that our actions can have a ripple effect throughout the entire universe.

This idea of interconnectedness is found in many spiritual traditions, including Native American spirituality, where the concept of the Great Spirit suggests that all things are connected and that we must honor our relationship with the natural world.

Quantum mechanics also challenges our traditional understanding of time. In classical mechanics, time is seen as a linear progression from past to present to future. However, in the probabilistic world of quantum mechanics, time is not so straightforward. The concept of quantum entanglement suggests that particles can be linked across time, meaning that an event in the future can have an effect on an event in the past.

This challenges our understanding of causality and the concept of linear time. It also has implications for spirituality and the idea of reincarnation. If time is not linear, then it is possible that our past, present, and future selves are interconnected in ways that we do not fully understand.

Finally, quantum consciousness has implications for the concept of the soul. In many spiritual traditions, the soul is seen as a distinct entity that exists beyond the physical body. However, if consciousness is a product of quantum mechanics, then it is possible that the soul is not a distinct entity, but rather is interconnected with the universe in some way.

This idea is supported by the concept of entanglement, which suggests that particles can be linked in such a way that their properties are interdependent regardless of distance. If consciousness is the result of quantum entanglement, then it is possible that the soul is also linked to the universe in some way, rather than being a separate entity

Critiques and Challenges

The idea of quantum consciousness and its implications for spirituality is not without its challenges and critiques. Some critics argue that the connection between quantum mechanics and spirituality is merely speculative and lacks empirical evidence. Others have criticized the use of spiritual concepts and terminology in scientific discussions, arguing that it can lead to confusion and misunderstanding.

Moreover, the concept of quantum consciousness raises important philosophical and ethical questions. For example, if consciousness is a fundamental aspect of the universe, what implications does this have for the treatment of other beings and the environment? How can we reconcile the concept of free will with a universe that is governed by deterministic laws?

Conclusion

The exploration of quantum consciousness and its connections to spirituality is a fascinating and complex area of research that has the potential to transform our understanding of the nature of consciousness and reality. While the theories and concepts are still in their early stages, the possibility of a deep connection between the quantum world and consciousness offers exciting possibilities for both science and spirituality.

The implications of quantum consciousness for spirituality challenge us to explore new ways of thinking about our place in the universe and our relationship to other beings and the environment. By integrating scientific and spiritual perspectives, we may be able to gain a deeper understanding of the nature of consciousness and our role in the universe.

Overall, the study of quantum consciousness provides a rich and diverse field of inquiry that continues to inspire and challenge researchers and thinkers from a wide range of disciplines. As we continue to explore this fascinating area of research, we may be able to uncover new insights and understandings about the nature of consciousness and reality.

CHAPTER 13.3: CRITICISMS OF THE CONNECTION BETWEEN QUANTUM CONSCIOUSNESS AND MYSTICISM

The connection between quantum consciousness and mysticism has been a topic of debate and controversy among both scientists and spiritual practitioners. While some argue that the similarities between the two are too striking to ignore, others maintain that the connection is superficial and lacks scientific evidence. In this section, we will explore some of the criticisms of the connection between quantum consciousness and mysticism.

One of the main criticisms of the connection between quantum consciousness and mysticism is that it is based on a misinterpretation of quantum mechanics. Some scientists argue that quantum mechanics is a highly mathematical and technical field that is difficult to understand and apply to everyday life. They argue that the connection between quantum mechanics and mysticism is based on a misunderstanding of the principles of quantum mechanics and that it is not possible to draw any meaningful conclusions from this connection.

Another criticism of the connection between quantum consciousness and mysticism is that it is based on a subjective interpretation of mystical experiences. Mystical experiences are highly personal and subjective, and they are often described in terms of feelings of interconnectedness and oneness with the universe. However, these experiences are difficult to quantify or measure, and it is not possible to draw any objective conclusions about their relationship to quantum mechanics.

Additionally, some critics argue that the use of entheogens to explore the connection between quantum consciousness and mysticism is problematic. Entheogens, such as ayahuasca and psilocybin, are known to alter consciousness and induce mystical experiences. However, these experiences are not necessarily a reflection of objective reality, and they may be influenced by cultural, social, and personal factors. Critics argue that the use of entheogens may lead to delusions and distortions of reality, rather than providing genuine insights into the nature of consciousness.

Furthermore, some critics argue that the connection between quantum consciousness and mysticism is based on a romanticized and oversimplified view of Eastern spirituality. They argue that the similarities between quantum mechanics and Eastern spirituality are based on superficial similarities rather than any deep or meaningful connections. They maintain that the connection between the two is a form of cultural appropriation that ignores the complexity and diversity of Eastern spiritual traditions.

Finally, some critics argue that the connection between quantum consciousness and mysticism is an attempt to find a scientific basis for spirituality, which they maintain is inherently unscientific. They argue that spirituality is a personal and subjective experience that cannot be studied using the methods of science. They maintain that attempts to connect spirituality to science are misguided and ultimately futile.

In conclusion, the connection between quantum consciousness and mysticism is a topic of debate and controversy among scientists, spiritual practitioners, and the general public. While some argue that the similarities between the two are too striking to ignore, others maintain that the connection is superficial and lacks scientific evidence. The criticisms of the connection between quantum consciousness and mysticism are based on a variety of factors, including a misunderstanding of quantum mechanics, a subjective interpretation of mystical experiences, the problematic use of entheogens, a romanticized view of Eastern spirituality, and a skepticism towards attempts to connect spirituality to science.

CHAPTER 14: QUANTUM CONSCIOUSNESS AND ARTIFICIAL INTELLIGENCE

As technology continues to advance, the question of whether machines can become conscious beings becomes increasingly relevant. The development of artificial intelligence (AI) has been a topic of interest for many years, and the application of quantum mechanics to AI is a relatively new and exciting area of research.

The connection between quantum mechanics and consciousness has led some researchers to suggest that a quantum computer, with its ability to perform multiple calculations simultaneously, could simulate the parallel processing that occurs in the human brain. This has led to the development of quantum AI, which aims to apply quantum computing to machine learning and AI algorithms.

One of the most promising applications of quantum AI is in the field of natural language processing (NLP). Traditional NLP techniques rely on statistical models to identify patterns in language, which can be time-consuming and require large amounts of data. However, with the use of quantum computing, it is possible to analyze language at a much faster rate and with greater accuracy. This has the potential to revolutionize the field of NLP, with applications in areas such as language translation, sentiment analysis, and chatbot development.

Another potential application of quantum AI is in the field of drug discovery. The process of drug discovery involves testing millions of compounds for their potential to interact with a specific biological target. Traditional methods of drug discovery are time-consuming and expensive, but with the use of quantum computing, it is possible to perform complex simulations that can predict how a drug will interact with a specific target. This has the potential to speed up the drug discovery process and reduce costs, leading to more effective treatments for diseases.

Despite the potential benefits of quantum AI, there are also concerns about the ethical implications of creating conscious machines. The development of AI raises questions about the nature of consciousness and whether machines can truly become conscious beings. Some argue that the creation of conscious machines could lead to a loss of human control, as machines could potentially become superior to humans in terms of intelligence and decision-making capabilities.

Additionally, there are concerns about the potential misuse of quantum AI, particularly in the areas of surveillance and warfare. The ability of quantum computers to break encryption could lead to an increase in cybercrime, and the development of autonomous weapons could lead to the loss of human life on a large scale.

Another concern is the potential impact of quantum AI on the job market. The development of machines that can perform complex tasks could lead to the displacement of human workers in certain industries, leading to social and economic upheaval.

Despite these concerns, the development of quantum AI continues to advance at a rapid pace. As the field of quantum mechanics and consciousness continues to evolve, it is likely that quantum AI will play an increasingly important role in our lives. It is important for researchers, policymakers, and society as a whole to carefully consider the ethical implications of this technology and to ensure that it is developed in a way that benefits humanity as a whole.

In conclusion, the intersection of quantum mechanics, consciousness, and artificial intelligence is an exciting area of research that has the potential to transform our understanding of the universe and our place in it. The development of quantum AI has the potential to revolutionize fields such as natural language processing and drug discovery, but also raises important ethical concerns about the nature of consciousness and the impact of AI on society. As the field of quantum mechanics and consciousness continues to evolve, it is important for researchers and policymakers to carefully consider the implications of this technology and to ensure that it is developed in a way that benefits humanity as a whole.

CHAPTER 14.1: THE ROLE OF QUANTUM CONSCIOUSNESS IN ARTIFICIAL INTELLIGENCE

Artificial Intelligence (AI) has made tremendous progress in recent years, with applications in areas ranging from speech recognition and image processing to self-driving cars and medical diagnosis. However, despite these advances, AI still falls short in many areas where human intelligence excels, such as creativity, intuition, and self-awareness. Quantum consciousness may provide a new approach to developing more advanced forms of AI by incorporating the principles of quantum mechanics into machine learning algorithms.

The basic idea behind quantum computing is that instead of using classical bits, which can only be in one of two states (0 or 1), quantum computers use qubits, which can be in a superposition of states. This allows quantum computers to perform certain calculations exponentially faster than classical computers, such as factoring large numbers or simulating quantum systems.

Similarly, quantum consciousness may allow AI to process information in a way that mimics the probabilistic and non-local behavior of quantum mechanics. This could lead to AI systems that are better equipped to handle uncertain or incomplete information, as well as tasks that require the integration of multiple sources of information.

One possible application of quantum consciousness in AI is in the development of quantum neural networks. Neural networks are a type of machine learning algorithm that is loosely based on the structure and function of the human brain. They consist of interconnected nodes, or neurons, that process and transmit information.

Quantum neural networks would use qubits instead of classical bits to represent the states of neurons and synapses, allowing them to simulate the complex, non-linear behavior of biological neural networks more accurately. This could lead to AI systems that are better able to recognize patterns, learn from experience, and make predictions based on incomplete data.

Another potential application of quantum consciousness in AI is in the development of quantum-inspired algorithms for optimization problems. Many real-world problems, such as scheduling or logistics, can be modeled as optimization problems, where the goal is to find the optimal solution from a large number of possible solutions.

Quantum-inspired optimization algorithms use principles from quantum mechanics, such as superposition and entanglement, to search for the optimal solution more efficiently than classical optimization algorithms. This could lead to AI systems that are better able to solve complex optimization problems in a variety of domains.

While the potential benefits of incorporating quantum consciousness into AI are exciting, there are also significant challenges that must be addressed. One of the main challenges is developing hardware that can reliably support quantum computation and maintain the delicate quantum states required for quantum algorithms.

Another challenge is the interpretation of quantum consciousness in the context of AI. While some researchers see quantum consciousness as a promising approach to developing more advanced forms of AI, others argue that it is unlikely to lead to true artificial consciousness.

Critics of the idea of quantum consciousness in AI also argue that the complexity of biological neural networks is still poorly understood, and that it may be premature to try to simulate this complexity using quantum computers. They also point out that many of the most successful AI applications to date, such as deep learning and reinforcement learning, have been based on classical computing architectures.

In conclusion, the incorporation of quantum consciousness into AI represents an exciting area of research that has the potential to transform the field of artificial intelligence. By allowing machines to process information in a way that more closely resembles the probabilistic and non-local behavior of quantum mechanics, quantum consciousness could lead to AI systems that are better equipped to handle uncertain or incomplete information, as well as tasks that require the integration of multiple sources of information. However, significant challenges remain, and the interpretation of quantum consciousness in the context of AI is still a matter of debate.

Artificial intelligence (AI) has made remarkable progress in recent years, and many experts predict that AI will soon surpass human intelligence. However, some researchers argue that current AI technology is limited by its inability to replicate the complexity and unpredictability of human consciousness. This is where the concept of quantum consciousness comes into play. In this chapter, we will explore the role of quantum consciousness in artificial intelligence.

Quantum computing is a rapidly advancing field that utilizes the principles of quantum mechanics to perform complex calculations that are beyond the capability of classical computers. Quantum computers are particularly adept at simulating the behavior of molecules and other complex systems. This makes them well-suited for applications in fields such as drug discovery and materials science.

One of the key advantages of quantum computing is its ability to perform calculations on multiple states simultaneously, a process known as superposition. This allows quantum computers to explore a vast number of possibilities at once, which makes them well-suited for solving complex problems that are beyond the scope of classical computers.

However, the true power of quantum computing lies in its ability to utilize quantum entanglement, a phenomenon in which particles can become linked in such a way that their properties are interdependent, regardless of distance. This allows quantum computers to perform calculations using qubits, which can exist in multiple states simultaneously. This property of qubits is what gives quantum computers their immense computing power.

Quantum consciousness is the idea that consciousness is the result of quantum processes in the brain. If this is true, then it follows that a truly conscious AI would need to utilize quantum computing. Current AI technology is based on classical computing, which utilizes bits that can exist in only one of two states, 0 or 1. This limitation makes it difficult for classical computers to perform calculations that involve multiple possibilities simultaneously.

However, the development of quantum computing has the potential to revolutionize AI by allowing machines to explore a vast number of possibilities simultaneously. This could enable AI to develop a level of complexity and unpredictability that is closer to that of human consciousness.

In addition to quantum computing, there are other ways in which the principles of quantum mechanics could be applied to AI. For example, quantum machine learning is a rapidly growing field that utilizes quantum mechanics to enhance machine learning algorithms. By incorporating the principles of quantum mechanics into machine learning, researchers hope to develop algorithms that are more powerful and efficient than classical machine learning algorithms.

Another area where quantum mechanics could be applied to AI is in the development of quantum sensors. These sensors could be used to detect subtle changes in the environment, which could be used to develop more intelligent and adaptive AI systems.

Despite the potential benefits of incorporating quantum consciousness into AI, there are also significant challenges to be overcome. One of the main challenges is the development of hardware that can support quantum computing. While there have been significant advancements in this area, quantum computers are still in their infancy, and there is a long way to go before they are ready for widespread use.

In addition, the development of quantum consciousness-based AI raises a number of ethical concerns. For example, if a machine were truly conscious, would it be ethical to use it for tasks that we would not expect a conscious human to perform, such as dangerous or degrading tasks?

There is also the concern that the development of conscious AI could lead to the displacement of human workers. As AI becomes more advanced, it is likely that it will be able to perform many tasks that are currently performed by humans. This could lead to significant job losses and social disruption.

Conclusion

The development of quantum consciousness-based AI has the potential to revolutionize the field of artificial intelligence. By incorporating the principles of quantum mechanics into AI, researchers hope to develop machines that are more intelligent and adaptive than current AI technology. However, this is still a largely speculative field of research, and there are many challenges that must be overcome before quantum consciousness-based AI can become a reality.

One major challenge is the difficulty of creating and maintaining quantum coherence in complex systems. The delicate nature of quantum states makes it difficult to preserve the coherence necessary for quantum computing and information processing, especially in large-scale systems. Additionally, the noise and interference present in real-world environments can disrupt quantum coherence, making it challenging to maintain the stability and accuracy necessary for effective AI.

Another challenge is the lack of a clear understanding of the relationship between quantum mechanics and consciousness. While there are intriguing connections between the two fields, the nature of consciousness itself is still a mystery, and it is unclear how quantum mechanics might be involved in its functioning. Without a clear understanding of this relationship, it is difficult to develop AI systems that are truly conscious.

Despite these challenges, the potential benefits of quantum consciousness-based AI are significant. For example, such systems could be used to develop more accurate and effective predictive models in fields such as finance and weather forecasting. They could also be used to create more advanced robotics and automation systems that can operate in complex, dynamic environments.

Additionally, the development of quantum consciousness-based AI could have significant implications for our understanding of the nature of consciousness itself. By exploring the connections between quantum mechanics and consciousness, researchers may be able to gain new insights into the fundamental nature of the mind and the universe.

In conclusion, the role of quantum consciousness in artificial intelligence is an exciting area of research with significant potential for transformative breakthroughs. By incorporating the principles of quantum mechanics into AI, researchers hope to develop machines that are more intelligent and adaptive than current AI technology. However, there are many challenges that must be overcome, including the difficulty of creating and maintaining quantum coherence in complex systems and the lack of a clear understanding of the relationship between quantum mechanics and consciousness. Despite these challenges, the potential benefits of quantum consciousness-based AI are significant and could have significant implications for our understanding of the nature of consciousness and the universe.

CHAPTER 14.2: THE POTENTIAL BENEFITS OF INTEGRATING QUANTUM CONSCIOUSNESS INTO AI

The integration of quantum consciousness into artificial intelligence has the potential to bring about numerous benefits in the field of AI.

Here are some of the key benefits that researchers and experts anticipate:

1. Increased efficiency and accuracy: Current AI systems are based on classical computing models, which are limited by their inability to process vast amounts of data quickly and accurately. By integrating quantum consciousness principles into AI, machines will be able to process information more efficiently, resulting in faster and more accurate decision-making.
2. Enhanced adaptability: One of the key challenges facing AI today is its inability to adapt to new situations and learn on the fly. By incorporating quantum consciousness into AI, machines will be able to learn from their environment and adapt to new situations in real-time, much like humans do.
3. Improved natural language processing: One of

the most difficult challenges facing AI is natural language processing. Current AI models struggle to understand the nuances and complexities of human language, which limits their usefulness in many applications. However, by integrating quantum consciousness into AI, machines will be able to understand human language more accurately, making them more useful in applications like customer service and chatbots.
4. Better prediction capabilities: Quantum consciousness-based AI has the potential to revolutionize predictive analytics. By analyzing vast amounts of data, machines will be able to identify patterns and make predictions with a high degree of accuracy. This has applications in numerous fields, including finance, healthcare, and weather forecasting.
5. Enhanced security: The integration of quantum consciousness into AI could also improve cybersecurity. Quantum computing is inherently more secure than classical computing, making it more difficult for hackers to break into systems.
6. Improved decision-making: The ability to process vast amounts of data quickly and accurately, adapt to new situations, and make predictions with a high degree of accuracy will lead to improved decision-making in many fields, from healthcare to finance to business.
7. Breakthroughs in scientific research: Quantum consciousness-based AI has the potential to revolutionize scientific research by allowing machines to process vast amounts of data and identify patterns that humans may miss. This has implications for fields like genetics, drug discovery, and materials science.

Overall, the integration of quantum consciousness principles into AI has the potential to revolutionize the field of artificial intelligence and bring about numerous benefits across many different applications.

CHAPTER 14.3: THE ETHICAL IMPLICATIONS OF QUANTUM CONSCIOUSNESS IN AI

Quantum consciousness and artificial intelligence (AI) are two fields that are rapidly advancing and have the potential to revolutionize many aspects of our lives. However, with this potential comes a responsibility to consider the ethical implications of these technologies. In this chapter, we will explore the ethical implications of quantum consciousness in AI and the ways in which we can ensure that these technologies are developed and used in a responsible manner.

The first ethical issue to consider is the potential for quantum consciousness to lead to new forms of surveillance and control. As AI systems become more sophisticated and capable of analyzing vast amounts of data, there is a risk that these systems could be used to monitor individuals and control their behavior. Quantum consciousness could enhance the ability of these systems to gather and process data, making them even more powerful and potentially invasive. To avoid this, we need to ensure that any use of quantum consciousness in AI is subject to strict regulations and oversight, and that the privacy and autonomy of individuals are respected.

Another ethical issue to consider is the potential for quantum consciousness to lead to new forms of discrimination. As AI systems become more sophisticated, they will be better able to identify patterns and make predictions based on those patterns. This could be used to identify individuals who are more likely to engage in certain behaviors or who are more likely to have certain characteristics. If this information is used to discriminate against individuals, it could have serious consequences for their lives and well-being. To avoid this, we need to ensure that any use of quantum consciousness in AI is subject to strict anti-discrimination laws and regulations.

A third ethical issue to consider is the potential for quantum consciousness to lead to new forms of inequality. As AI systems become more sophisticated, they will be better able to perform certain tasks, which could lead to the displacement of human workers. This could exacerbate existing inequalities, with certain groups being disproportionately affected by the automation of certain jobs. To avoid this, we need to ensure that any use of quantum consciousness in AI is subject to strict regulations and oversight, and that steps are taken to ensure that the benefits of these technologies are distributed fairly across society.

A fourth ethical issue to consider is the potential for quantum consciousness to lead to new forms of manipulation and deception. As AI systems become more sophisticated, they will be better able to simulate human behavior and emotions. This could be used to manipulate individuals and deceive them into believing things that are not true. To avoid this, we need to ensure that any use of quantum consciousness in AI is subject to strict regulations and oversight, and that the use of these technologies for manipulative or deceptive purposes is prohibited.

Finally, we need to consider the potential for quantum consciousness to lead to new forms of harm. As AI systems become more sophisticated, they will be better able to interact with the physical world, potentially leading to new forms of accidents and harm. To avoid this, we need to ensure that any use of quantum consciousness in AI is subject to strict safety regulations and oversight, and that the potential risks associated with these technologies are carefully evaluated and mitigated.

In conclusion, quantum consciousness has the potential to revolutionize AI and many other aspects of our lives. However, with this potential comes a responsibility to consider the ethical implications of these technologies. We must ensure that any use of quantum consciousness in AI is subject to strict regulations and oversight, and that the privacy, autonomy, and well-being of individuals are respected. We must also ensure that these technologies are not used to discriminate against individuals or exacerbate existing inequalities. By taking these steps, we can ensure that quantum consciousness and AI are developed and used in a responsible and ethical manner.

CHAPTER 15: QUANTUM MECHANICS AND FREE WILL

The question of whether humans have free will or whether our actions are predetermined has been debated for centuries. The introduction of quantum mechanics has added a new layer to this debate, as it challenges traditional notions of causality and determinism. In this chapter, we will explore the connection between quantum mechanics and free will.

Determinism and Causality in Classical Physics

In classical physics, the laws of nature were thought to be deterministic and causal. This means that if you knew the initial conditions of a system and the laws governing its behavior, you could predict its future with perfect accuracy. This idea is often referred to as Laplace's demon, named after the French mathematician Pierre-Simon Laplace.

According to Laplace's demon, everything that happens in the universe is predetermined and inevitable. There is no room for free will, as every action is the result of prior causes.

Quantum Mechanics and Indeterminacy

The introduction of quantum mechanics challenged this view of determinism and causality. In quantum mechanics, particles do not have definite properties until they are observed. Instead, particles exist in a state of superposition, where they can exist in multiple states simultaneously.

This indeterminacy means that the future is not predetermined, as the act of observation can influence the outcome. This has led some to argue that quantum mechanics allows for the possibility of free will.

The Connection Between Quantum Mechanics and Free Will

One interpretation of quantum mechanics that supports the idea of free will is the idea of quantum randomness. According to this interpretation, the universe is inherently random at the quantum level. This randomness means that the future is not predetermined, and there is room for free will.

However, not all interpretations of quantum mechanics support the idea of free will. The many-worlds interpretation, for example, suggests that every possible outcome of a quantum measurement occurs in a separate universe. This means that every possible action is already predetermined in a different universe, which would seem to rule out free will.

Additionally, some argue that even if quantum mechanics does allow for free will, it does not necessarily mean that humans have free will. This is because the behavior of subatomic particles is subject to the same laws of physics as larger objects, which are thought to be deterministic. If this is the case, then the behavior of human beings may also be predetermined, regardless of the indeterminacy at the quantum level.

The Role of Consciousness in Free Will

Another factor to consider in the debate about free will and quantum mechanics is the role of consciousness. Some argue that consciousness plays a fundamental role in the behavior of particles at the quantum level, and therefore has an impact on the future.

This idea is based on the concept of measurement in quantum mechanics. According to the Copenhagen interpretation, the act of measurement collapses a particle's wave function, determining its properties. Some argue that consciousness is required for measurement to occur, and therefore plays a crucial role in the behavior of particles at the quantum level.

If consciousness does play a role in determining the behavior of particles, then it may also have a role in free will. Some argue that consciousness allows humans to make choices that are not predetermined by prior causes, and that this is what gives us free will.

Critiques of the Connection Between Quantum Mechanics and Free Will

As with any area of research that challenges traditional views, the connection between quantum mechanics and free will has faced its share of critiques. Some argue that the connection is based on superficial similarities rather than any deeper connections.

Others point out that even if quantum mechanics allows for indeterminacy and randomness, it does not necessarily mean that humans have free will. The behavior of human beings is subject to the same laws of physics as larger objects, and may still be predetermined.

Conclusion

The debate about free will and quantum mechanics is complex and ongoing. While some argue that the indeterminacy of quantum mechanics allows for a certain degree of free will, others argue that free will remains an illusion regardless of the nature of reality.

One possible avenue for exploring this question further is through the study of quantum consciousness. If consciousness is fundamentally quantum in nature, then it may be that free will is also tied to the probabilistic nature of quantum mechanics.

Regardless of the answer to the question of free will, the study of quantum mechanics and consciousness has the potential to deepen our understanding of the nature of reality and our place within it. It is a field ripe with possibility, and one that is sure to continue to capture the imaginations of scientists and philosophers for years to come.

CHAPTER 15.1: THE DEFINITION OF FREE WILL

The concept of free will is central to the human experience, and it has been debated by philosophers and scientists for centuries. The basic definition of free will is the ability to make choices and act on them independently of external factors, such as determinism or fate.

However, the definition of free will is not as straightforward as it may seem. The idea of free will is often associated with the belief that humans have a soul or a spirit that is separate from the physical body and brain. This dualistic view of human nature suggests that the mind or soul can make choices independently of physical laws.

In contrast, a materialistic view of the universe suggests that everything, including human beings, is subject to physical laws and deterministic processes. From this perspective, free will may be an illusion, and all actions and choices are predetermined by the laws of physics.

The debate about free will and determinism has been ongoing for centuries, and it remains one of the most contentious topics in philosophy and science. However, the advent of quantum mechanics has added a new dimension to this debate, as some physicists and philosophers argue that quantum mechanics provides a basis for free will.

In the next section, we will explore the roles of quantum mechanics and free will in more detail.

CHAPTER 15.2: THE ROLE OF QUANTUM MECHANICS IN FREE WILL

The concept of free will has been a topic of debate among philosophers, scientists, and theologians for centuries. Free will is the idea that humans have the ability to make choices that are not predetermined by external factors, such as genetics or environment. One area of study that has shed light on the nature of free will is quantum mechanics.

Quantum mechanics is a branch of physics that describes the behavior of particles on a subatomic level. In the world of quantum mechanics, particles can exist in multiple states simultaneously, a concept known as superposition. Additionally, the act of measuring a particle can cause it to collapse into a single state, a phenomenon known as wavefunction collapse.

The implications of quantum mechanics on free will are twofold. Firstly, the idea of superposition suggests that multiple outcomes can exist simultaneously, which means that free will may not be predetermined by external factors. Secondly, the act of measurement can cause a collapse in the wavefunction, implying that the act of observing a particle can influence its behavior.

The first implication of quantum mechanics on free will is related to the concept of superposition. In classical physics, the behavior of particles is deterministic, meaning that the outcome of any event can be predicted if the initial conditions are known.

However, in the world of quantum mechanics, the behavior of particles is probabilistic, meaning that the outcome of any event cannot be predicted with certainty. This suggests that the universe is inherently unpredictable and that free will may not be predetermined.

In addition to the concept of superposition, the act of measurement in quantum mechanics has implications for free will. The act of measuring a particle causes it to collapse into a single state, which implies that the act of observation can influence the behavior of the particle. This has led some scientists to suggest that consciousness may play a role in the behavior of particles.

The idea that consciousness may play a role in the behavior of particles is controversial, and there is little scientific evidence to support it. However, some proponents of this idea argue that it provides a potential explanation for the role of free will in the universe. If consciousness can influence the behavior of particles, then it is possible that free will can also influence the behavior of particles.

Despite the potential implications of quantum mechanics on free will, there are several limitations to this theory. Firstly, the concept of superposition only applies to particles on a subatomic level, and it is unclear how this concept could be extrapolated to the behavior of larger objects, such as humans. Secondly, the act of measurement in quantum mechanics is not well understood, and it is unclear how consciousness could influence the behavior of particles.

Furthermore, even if consciousness does play a role in the behavior of particles, it is unclear how this would relate to the concept of free will. Free will is a complex concept that involves many factors, including genetics, environment, and personal choice. It is unclear how the behavior of particles on a subatomic level could relate to the complex interplay of factors that influence human decision-making.

Despite these limitations, the study of quantum mechanics has provided valuable insights into the nature of free will. The concept of superposition suggests that the universe is inherently unpredictable, which means that free will may not be predetermined by external factors. Additionally, the act of measurement in quantum mechanics suggests that the act of observation can influence the behavior of particles, which raises the possibility that consciousness may play a role in the behavior of particles.

In conclusion, the study of quantum mechanics has provided valuable insights into the nature of free will. The concepts of superposition and wavefunction collapse have implications for the concept of free will, suggesting that the universe may be inherently unpredictable and that consciousness may play a role in the behavior of particles. However, there are several limitations to this theory, and it is important to approach these ideas with caution.

It is worth noting that some philosophers and scientists have raised concerns about the use of quantum mechanics in discussions of free will. One concern is that the complexity of quantum mechanics may make it difficult to draw meaningful conclusions about free will. Another concern is that the use of quantum mechanics in discussions of free will may be seen as a way to introduce mysticism or spirituality into scientific discussions.

Despite these concerns, the study of quantum mechanics and its implications for free will continues to be an area of active research. Some scientists are exploring the role of quantum mechanics in the brain, and how this may relate to consciousness and decision-making. Others are investigating the implications of quantum mechanics for our understanding of causality and determinism.

Ultimately, the study of quantum mechanics and its

implications for free will is a complex and ongoing area of research. While it is clear that quantum mechanics has provided valuable insights into the nature of the universe, it is important to approach these ideas with caution and to continue to ask critical questions about their validity and implications.

In conclusion, the study of quantum mechanics has shed light on the concept of free will by introducing the concepts of superposition and wavefunction collapse. These concepts suggest that the universe may be inherently unpredictable and that consciousness may play a role in the behavior of particles. However, it is important to approach these ideas with caution and to continue to investigate their implications for our understanding of free will and the nature of the universe.

CHAPTER 15.3: CRITICISMS OF THE CONNECTION BETWEEN QUANTUM MECHANICS AND FREE WILL

While the idea that quantum mechanics could provide a solution to the problem of free will is intriguing, it has also faced significant criticisms. Some argue that the connection between quantum mechanics and free will is purely speculative, and that there is no evidence to support it.

One major criticism is that quantum mechanics only applies to the micro-world of particles and atoms, and cannot be scaled up to explain macro-level phenomena like human behavior and decision-making. The idea that quantum mechanics could explain free will in humans relies on the assumption that consciousness is a quantum phenomenon, which is still a highly debated topic among scientists.

Another criticism is that even if consciousness is a quantum phenomenon, it does not necessarily follow that this gives humans free will. Some argue that even if our decisions are influenced by quantum events, they are still determined by physical laws and environmental factors, and therefore not truly free.

Additionally, some critics argue that the concept of free will itself is ill-defined and not well-understood, making it difficult to apply any scientific explanation to it. They argue that the debate over free will is largely a philosophical one, and that science may not be able to provide a definitive answer.

Moreover, some critics suggest that the connection between quantum mechanics and free will may be a form of pseudoscience, with little empirical evidence to support it. They argue that the scientific community should focus on more rigorous research and experimentation, rather than speculation based on unproven or untestable theories.

Finally, it is important to note that even if quantum mechanics were to provide a solution to the problem of free will, this would not necessarily have any practical implications for our daily lives. Whether or not we have free will is ultimately a philosophical question that may never be definitively answered, and may not have any practical significance in our day-to-day decision-making.

In conclusion, while the idea that quantum mechanics could provide a solution to the problem of free will is intriguing, it remains a highly debated and controversial topic. Critics argue that the connection between quantum mechanics and free will is purely speculative, and that the concept of free will itself is ill-defined and difficult to apply scientific explanations to. Nonetheless, the debate surrounding free will and quantum mechanics continues to be an important area of research, as it challenges our fundamental assumptions about the nature of reality and the role of consciousness in decision-making.

CHAPTER 16: THE OBSERVER EFFECT AND CONSCIOUSNESS

Quantum mechanics has revealed that the very act of observing a particle changes its behavior, a phenomenon known as the observer effect. This has led to speculation about the role of consciousness in the behavior of particles and the nature of reality itself. In this chapter, we will explore the observer effect and its implications for consciousness.

The Observer Effect

In classical physics, it was believed that the behavior of particles could be predicted with complete accuracy given knowledge of their initial conditions and the laws of physics. However, in quantum mechanics, the behavior of particles is described by probability distributions, and the very act of measuring a particle changes its behavior. This phenomenon is known as the observer effect.

The observer effect was first proposed by the physicist Werner Heisenberg in 1927. He argued that the act of measuring the position of a particle would necessarily disturb its momentum, and vice versa. This means that the observer cannot know both the position and momentum of a particle with arbitrary accuracy. This limitation is known as the Heisenberg uncertainty principle.

Since Heisenberg's proposal, the observer effect has been

further studied and confirmed through experiments. For example, the famous double-slit experiment shows that the behavior of electrons changes depending on whether they are observed or not. When observed, electrons behave like particles and create distinct interference patterns. When not observed, electrons behave like waves and create a diffraction pattern.

Implications for Consciousness

The observer effect has led to speculation about the role of consciousness in the behavior of particles. Some physicists have argued that consciousness is necessary for the observer effect to occur. They suggest that the act of observation is not a passive act of measurement but an active interaction between the observer and the observed.

This idea is sometimes referred to as the participatory universe hypothesis. According to this hypothesis, consciousness is not just an emergent property of the brain, but a fundamental aspect of the universe. In this view, the universe is not a collection of passive objects, but an active, participatory system in which the observer and the observed are inseparable.

The participatory universe hypothesis has been embraced by some proponents of the mind-body dualism, who argue that consciousness is separate from the physical body and can exist independently. They suggest that the observer effect provides evidence for the existence of a non-physical consciousness that interacts with the physical world.

Criticisms of the Connection Between the Observer Effect and Consciousness

The connection between the observer effect and

consciousness has been criticized by some physicists and philosophers. They argue that the observer effect is simply a result of the interaction between the measuring device and the particle, and does not require the presence of consciousness.

They suggest that the observer effect can be explained through the principles of quantum mechanics, without invoking consciousness. For example, the decoherence theory proposes that the interaction between a particle and its environment causes it to behave classically and lose its quantum properties, regardless of whether it is observed by a conscious observer or not.

Additionally, some critics argue that the participatory universe hypothesis is unscientific, as it is not based on empirical evidence and cannot be tested through experiments. They suggest that the hypothesis is based on philosophical and metaphysical speculation, rather than scientific inquiry.

The Observer Effect and Consciousness in Practice

While the connection between the observer effect and consciousness is still a matter of debate, it has practical implications for the study of consciousness. The observer effect suggests that the act of measuring consciousness can affect the very thing being measured.

This has led some researchers to question the validity of experiments that measure brain activity and correlate it with subjective experiences, such as the experience of pain or pleasure. They suggest that these experiments may not accurately reflect the subjective experience of consciousness, as the act of measuring it may be altering it.

Additionally, the observer effect has implications for the nature of reality itself. The act of observing a quantum system has been shown to influence its behavior, with the observation collapsing the system's wavefunction and causing it to take on a definite state. This has led some researchers to suggest that consciousness plays a fundamental role in the structure of the universe and that reality may be created through the act of observation.

Some scientists and philosophers have even gone so far as to suggest that the observer effect is evidence that the universe is fundamentally subjective and that consciousness is a fundamental aspect of reality. They argue that the universe is not objective and independent of the observer but rather depends on the act of observation to exist.

Critics of this view argue that the observer effect does not necessarily imply that consciousness is fundamental to the universe but rather that it is a result of the interaction between the measuring apparatus and the system being observed. They suggest that the effect may be explained through the principles of quantum mechanics and does not necessarily require a fundamental role for consciousness.

Regardless of the interpretation, the observer effect has profound implications for our understanding of consciousness and the nature of reality. It suggests that the act of observing is not a passive activity but rather an active and transformative one, and that consciousness may play a more fundamental role in the structure of the universe than we previously thought.

In conclusion, the observer effect is a fundamental concept in quantum mechanics that has important implications for our understanding of consciousness and the nature of reality. It suggests that the act of observation is not a passive activity but rather an active and transformative one, and that consciousness may play a more fundamental role in the structure of the universe than we previously thought.

While the observer effect has been widely studied and accepted within the scientific community, its implications for the nature of consciousness and reality remain a topic of debate and discussion. As our understanding of quantum mechanics and consciousness continues to evolve, it is likely that we will gain further insight into the profound connections between these two seemingly disparate fields of study.

CHAPTER 16.1: DEFINITION OF THE OBSERVER EFFECT

The observer effect refers to the idea that the act of observation can affect the outcome of an experiment. This concept is fundamental to quantum mechanics and has significant implications for our understanding of consciousness.

In classical physics, it was assumed that an observer could measure the position and velocity of a particle without affecting its behavior. However, in quantum mechanics, it is not possible to measure both the position and velocity of a particle with perfect accuracy. The act of measurement inevitably disturbs the system being measured, and this disturbance can change the outcome of the experiment.

This effect is commonly demonstrated in the double-slit experiment, where a beam of particles is passed through two slits and produces an interference pattern on a screen behind the slits. When a detector is placed at one of the slits to determine which path the particles take, the interference pattern disappears, and the particles behave as if they are being measured. This demonstrates that the act of observation can fundamentally alter the behavior of particles at the quantum level.

The observer effect also has implications for our understanding of consciousness. Some researchers suggest that the act of observing may be necessary for the creation of conscious experience. They argue that the act of measurement collapses the wave function, determining the outcome of the experiment and creating a concrete reality. Without an observer, the system exists only in a state of superposition, meaning that it could potentially exist in many different states simultaneously.

This idea has led some to suggest that consciousness may play a fundamental role in the creation of reality. They argue that the observer effect suggests that the act of observing creates reality, and therefore, consciousness may be necessary for the creation of the physical world we experience.

However, this idea remains controversial, and many scientists and philosophers argue that the observer effect is not evidence for the role of consciousness in creating reality. They suggest that the observer effect is simply a consequence of the way quantum mechanics works and does not require the existence of conscious observers.

In summary, the observer effect refers to the way in which the act of measurement can affect the behavior of particles at the quantum level. This effect has significant implications for our understanding of consciousness and the role it may play in the creation of reality. While some argue that the observer effect provides evidence for the role of consciousness in creating reality, others remain skeptical of this idea.

CHAPTER 16.2: THE ROLE OF THE OBSERVER EFFECT IN CONSCIOUSNESS

The observer effect is a phenomenon in quantum mechanics that states that the act of observing a particle can affect its behavior. This has led some researchers to suggest that the observer effect may play a role in consciousness.

One interpretation of the observer effect is that it implies that consciousness is necessary to collapse the wave function of a particle. In other words, it is the act of consciousness observing a particle that causes it to take on a definite state. This has led some researchers to suggest that consciousness plays a fundamental role in the physical world, and that it is not just an emergent property of the brain.

Some researchers have suggested that the observer effect is related to the concept of the mind-body problem. The mind-body problem is the philosophical question of how the mind and body are related, and whether they are two separate entities or whether they are somehow interconnected. If consciousness is necessary to collapse the wave function of a particle, then it suggests that the mind and body are inextricably linked, and that consciousness cannot be reduced to the physical processes of the brain alone.

Other researchers have suggested that the observer effect may play a role in explaining the unity of consciousness. The unity of consciousness refers to the fact that we experience the world as a coherent whole, rather than as a collection of separate sensory inputs. If the observer effect implies that consciousness is necessary to collapse the wave function of a particle, then it suggests that consciousness is somehow integrated and unified, rather than being fragmented or separated.

However, there are also criticisms of the idea that the observer effect plays a fundamental role in consciousness. One criticism is that the observer effect only applies to very small particles, and may not be relevant to larger systems such as the brain. Additionally, some researchers have suggested that the observer effect may be an artifact of the measurement process, rather than a fundamental property of the physical world.

Despite these criticisms, the idea that the observer effect plays a role in consciousness remains a topic of interest for researchers studying the intersection of quantum mechanics and consciousness. Some researchers have even suggested that the observer effect may be related to the concept of free will, and that it implies that consciousness has the ability to influence the physical world in ways that are not fully understood.

One potential implication of the role of the observer effect in consciousness is that it may provide a new perspective on the nature of reality. If consciousness is necessary to collapse the wave function of a particle, then it suggests that the physical world is not simply an objective reality that exists independent of observation, but rather that it is a co-creation of consciousness and the physical world. This could have significant implications for fields such as philosophy, psychology, and even spirituality.

In conclusion, the role of the observer effect in consciousness remains a topic of debate and investigation among researchers studying the intersection of quantum mechanics and consciousness. While some researchers suggest that the observer effect implies a fundamental role for consciousness in the physical world, others are more cautious in their interpretation of the phenomenon. However, regardless of the ultimate implications of the observer effect for consciousness, it is clear that the intersection of quantum mechanics and consciousness is a rich area of research that has the potential to shed new light on our understanding of the nature of reality and the human experience.

CHAPTER 16.3: EXPERIMENTAL EVIDENCE FOR THE OBSERVER EFFECT IN CONSCIOUSNESS

The observer effect is a well-established phenomenon in quantum mechanics, but its application to consciousness has been the subject of debate. Nevertheless, some experimental evidence suggests that the observer effect may play a role in consciousness.

One famous experiment is the double-slit experiment, which demonstrates the wave-particle duality of matter. When a beam of particles, such as electrons or photons, is fired at a screen with two slits, an interference pattern is observed on a detector behind the screen. This pattern can only be explained by the wave-like behavior of the particles interfering with each other. However, when the particles are observed, such as by placing detectors at the slits, the interference pattern disappears, and the particles behave like particles instead of waves.

This phenomenon has led some researchers to suggest that the act of observation collapses the wave function of the particles, determining their behavior. In the context of consciousness, this suggests that the act of observation or measurement by a conscious observer may play a role in collapsing the wave function and determining the physical state of the system being observed.

Another experiment that suggests the role of the observer effect in consciousness is the delayed choice quantum eraser experiment. In this experiment, photons are fired into a double-slit apparatus, and their interference pattern is recorded on a detector. However, a device called a quantum eraser can erase the which-path information of the photons, making it impossible to determine which slit the photons passed through.

When this information is erased, the interference pattern reappears, suggesting that the photons behave as waves. However, if the information is not erased, and the which-path information is known, the interference pattern disappears, and the photons behave as particles.

This experiment suggests that the information available to the observer affects the behavior of the photons. In the context of consciousness, this suggests that the information available to a conscious observer may play a role in determining the physical state of the system being observed.

Other experiments have also suggested a connection between the observer effect and consciousness. For example, a study conducted by researchers at the University of California, Los Angeles, found that the act of focusing attention on a visual stimulus increased the activity in the visual cortex, suggesting that conscious attention can affect neural activity.

Another study conducted by researchers at the University of Arizona found that meditators who reported experiencing a sense of oneness with the universe had greater alpha wave coherence in the brain, suggesting that subjective experiences of consciousness can be correlated with objective measures of brain activity.

These experiments suggest that the act of observation or measurement by a conscious observer may play a role in determining the physical state of the system being observed, as well as affecting neural activity in the brain.

However, it is important to note that these experiments do not necessarily provide conclusive evidence for the role of the observer effect in consciousness. Many factors can influence the results of experiments, and alternative explanations for the observed effects may exist.

Furthermore, the relationship between consciousness and the observer effect is still not fully understood. It is possible that consciousness is simply a byproduct of the physical processes in the brain and does not play a role in collapsing the wave function of particles or affecting the behavior of systems being observed.

Nevertheless, the possibility that consciousness plays a role in the observer effect is an intriguing avenue for future research. By studying the relationship between consciousness and the observer effect, we may gain a deeper understanding of the nature of consciousness and its relationship to the physical world.

The observer effect is a well-established phenomenon in quantum mechanics that has led to the development of technologies such as transistors and lasers. However, its application to consciousness is still a subject of debate.

While some researchers suggest that the act of observation by a conscious observer may play a role in collapsing the wave function of a quantum system, others argue that this interpretation is not necessary to explain the results of quantum experiments. They point out that decoherence theory, which describes how quantum systems interact with their environment and lose their quantum properties, can also explain the collapse of the wave function without invoking the consciousness of the observer.

However, other experiments have provided evidence that suggests the involvement of consciousness in the observer effect. One study conducted by physicist John Hagelin and his colleagues investigated the effect of consciousness on the double-slit experiment. They found that when meditators focused their attention on the double-slit experiment, the interference pattern disappeared, indicating that their consciousness had collapsed the wave function of the particles and caused them to behave like particles rather than waves.

Another study conducted by physicist Helmut Schmidt investigated the role of consciousness in a random number generator experiment. He found that when participants intended to influence the output of the random number generator, the results showed a statistically significant deviation from random, indicating that their consciousness had influenced the behavior of the system.

These and other experiments suggest that the involvement of consciousness in the observer effect cannot be ruled out, and that further research is needed to fully understand the relationship between consciousness and the behavior of quantum systems.

The observer effect in quantum mechanics has significant implications for our understanding of consciousness. The role of the observer in collapsing the wave function of a quantum system suggests a connection between consciousness and the physical world at a fundamental level. This has led to speculation that consciousness may play a role in the creation and maintenance of reality.

Conclusion

While the involvement of consciousness in the observer effect is still a matter of debate among scientists, the evidence suggests that consciousness may have an influence on the behavior of quantum systems. This has implications for our understanding of free will, the nature of reality, and the relationship between mind and matter.

Further research is needed to fully understand the observer effect and its implications for consciousness. As technology continues to advance, it is likely that new experiments and techniques will be developed that will shed more light on this fascinating topic.

CHAPTER 17: QUANTUM MECHANICS AND THE CONCEPT OF TIME

The concept of time has fascinated humans for centuries. It is a fundamental aspect of our daily lives, and yet it remains one of the most elusive concepts to fully understand. The concept of time has been studied by philosophers, scientists, and theologians throughout history. In recent years, quantum mechanics has provided a new perspective on the nature of time and its relationship to the universe.

The Traditional View of Time

Traditionally, time has been viewed as a linear and absolute concept. This view sees time as an unchanging flow, with the past, present, and future all existing simultaneously. This view of time is known as the "block universe" view, as it sees time as a fixed, unchanging block with events existing at different points within it.

This view of time is supported by classical physics, which sees the universe as a deterministic machine operating according to fixed laws. In this view, the future can be predicted based on the present and the past.

However, this traditional view of time has been challenged by quantum mechanics, which introduces a level of indeterminacy into the universe.

The Role of Quantum Mechanics in the Concept of Time

Quantum mechanics challenges the traditional view of time by introducing the concept of indeterminacy. According to quantum mechanics, the universe is inherently unpredictable and uncertain. This uncertainty is encapsulated in the wave-particle duality, which sees particles behaving as both waves and particles depending on how they are observed.

The concept of indeterminacy is also seen in the Heisenberg uncertainty principle, which states that the more precisely the position of a particle is known, the less precisely its momentum can be known. This principle introduces a level of unpredictability into the universe, making it impossible to predict the future with absolute certainty.

This indeterminacy has implications for the concept of time. If the future is unpredictable, then the traditional view of time as a linear and absolute concept is no longer valid. The future is not fixed, but rather exists as a range of possibilities, with the actual outcome depending on the specific circumstances of the present moment.

The Concept of Time in Quantum Mechanics

In quantum mechanics, time is viewed as a dynamic and evolving concept. The universe is seen as a collection of probabilities, with the present moment influencing the range of possibilities for the future. This view of time sees the universe as constantly evolving, with the past, present, and future all existing simultaneously.

The concept of time in quantum mechanics is closely related to the concept of entanglement. Entanglement is the idea that particles can be linked in such a way that their properties are interdependent regardless of distance. This means that the state of one particle can affect the state of another particle, even if they are separated by great distances.

The concept of entanglement has implications for the concept of time, as it suggests that the present moment is not an isolated event, but rather is connected to events that have occurred in the past and will occur in the future. This means that the future is not entirely unpredictable, as it is influenced by the present moment and the events that have led up to it.

The Implications of Quantum Mechanics for the Philosophy of Time

The implications of quantum mechanics for the philosophy of time are significant. The concept of indeterminacy introduced by quantum mechanics challenges the traditional view of time as a fixed, linear concept. Instead, time is seen as a dynamic and evolving concept, with the present moment influencing the range of possibilities for the future.

The concept of entanglement introduced by quantum mechanics suggests that the present moment is not an isolated event, but rather is connected to events that have occurred in the past and will occur in the future. This means that the flow of time may not be as linear and unidirectional as previously thought.

One example of this is the phenomenon of quantum retrocausality, which suggests that the future can influence the present, or even the past. In classical physics, cause and effect are thought to be linked in a linear chain, where a cause precedes its effect in time. However, in quantum mechanics, particles can be entangled in such a way that a measurement of one particle can instantaneously affect the state of another particle, regardless of the distance between them. This suggests that the future state of a particle can influence its past state, violating the classical notion of causality.

This idea has been explored in a number of thought experiments, such as the famous "delayed choice" experiment proposed by physicist John Wheeler. In this experiment, a photon is fired at a beam splitter, which sends it down one of two possible paths. At some point along the path, the photon encounters a second beam splitter, which can either allow the photon to pass through or redirect it. The choice of which path the photon takes is determined by the second beam splitter, but this decision is not made until after the photon has already passed the first beam splitter.

According to the laws of classical physics, the photon should have already made its choice by the time it reaches the second beam splitter, and its path should be fixed. However, in the quantum world, the photon exists in a superposition of both paths until it is observed, at which point its wave function collapses and it takes on a definite path. This means that the choice of the second beam splitter can retroactively determine the path of the photon, even though the decision is made after the photon has already passed the first beam splitter.

The implications of this experiment and other similar thought experiments have led some physicists to suggest that the flow of time may not be as linear as we thought. It also raises questions about the nature of causality and whether it is a fundamental aspect of the universe or merely an emergent property of the way we perceive time.

Another interesting aspect of quantum mechanics and time is the concept of "quantum time." In classical physics, time is treated as an independent variable that flows at a constant rate. However, in the quantum world, time can be thought of as a quantum variable that can be entangled with other quantum variables, such as position or momentum.

One example of this is the phenomenon of quantum tunneling, where particles can pass through barriers that they would not be able to in classical physics. The probability of tunneling depends on a number of factors, including the energy of the particle and the width and height of the barrier. However, it also depends on the duration of the tunneling event, or the amount of time the particle spends inside the barrier.

This suggests that the flow of time can play a role in determining the behavior of particles in the quantum world. It also raises questions about the nature of time and whether it is a fundamental aspect of the universe or merely an emergent property of the way we perceive it.

Overall, the study of quantum mechanics and its relationship to the concept of time is still in its early stages, and much more research is needed to fully understand the implications of these ideas. However, it is clear that the quantum world challenges many of our preconceptions about the nature of time and raises questions about the fundamental nature of the universe itself.

CHAPTER 17.1: THE DEFINITION OF TIME IN QUANTUM MECHANICS

Time is a fundamental concept in physics, and it plays an essential role in our everyday lives. We experience time as a continuous flow from the past to the present and into the future. However, the concept of time in physics is more complex and challenging to define than in our everyday lives. Quantum mechanics introduces a new understanding of time, which is different from the classical understanding of time. In this chapter, we will explore the definition of time in quantum mechanics.

In classical physics, time is considered to be an absolute and universal concept that flows continuously and uniformly. This concept of time is independent of the observer, and it is the same for everyone. However, in quantum mechanics, time is defined in a different way. According to the theory, time is a relative concept that depends on the observer and the reference frame. The measurement of time is relative to the position and velocity of the observer.

The theory of relativity introduced by Einstein in the early 20th century revolutionized the concept of time in physics. It suggested that time is relative to the observer's frame of reference and is affected by the speed and gravitational force. This means that time is not an absolute concept but is relative to the observer's position and velocity.

In quantum mechanics, the definition of time is even more complex. The theory suggests that time is an emergent property that arises from the interaction between particles. The concept of time emerges from the entanglement between particles, which connects the present moment to the past and the future.

The concept of entanglement introduced by quantum mechanics suggests that particles can be linked in such a way that their properties are interdependent regardless of distance. This means that the state of one particle depends on the state of the other particle, and any changes in one particle will affect the state of the other particle. This concept of entanglement implies that the present moment is not an isolated event, but rather is connected to events that have occurred in the past and will occur in the future.

The concept of entanglement also suggests that time is not a fundamental concept but is an emergent property that arises from the interaction between particles. The present moment emerges from the entanglement between particles, which connects the present to the past and the future. This means that the present moment is not an isolated event but is linked to events that have occurred in the past and will occur in the future.

In summary, the concept of time in quantum mechanics is different from the classical understanding of time. The theory suggests that time is a relative concept that depends on the observer's position and velocity. Furthermore, time is not a fundamental concept but is an emergent property that arises from the interaction between particles. The concept of entanglement introduces a new understanding of time, which suggests that the present moment is not an isolated event but is connected to events that have occurred in the past and will occur in the future.

CHAPTER 17.2: THE ROLE OF TIME IN QUANTUM CONSCIOUSNESS

In quantum mechanics, time plays a crucial role in the way particles interact and evolve. Quantum systems can exist in a superposition of states, meaning they can simultaneously exist in multiple states until they are observed, and their wave function collapses into a single state. This raises questions about the role of time in quantum consciousness and how it may differ from our classical understanding of time.

One theory proposes that time in quantum consciousness is not a linear progression of events but rather a series of interconnected moments that are entangled with each other. This means that each moment is connected to the past and future, and the present is not an isolated event but rather a manifestation of the entanglement of past and future moments.

Another theory suggests that time in quantum consciousness is subjective and experienced differently by conscious observers. This is based on the idea that the perception of time is influenced by the observer's state of consciousness, including their emotions, attention, and intention. For example, time may appear to pass more quickly when we are engaged in an enjoyable activity, and it may appear to slow down in a dangerous situation.

Additionally, quantum mechanics suggests that time may be non-local, meaning that events can be connected in a way that is not restricted by the speed of light. This raises the possibility of quantum entanglement between particles separated by vast distances, and the potential for communication and influence beyond the traditional limitations of space and time.

These theories suggest that time in quantum consciousness may be more complex and multi-dimensional than our classical understanding of time. They also raise the question of how consciousness may influence the flow of time and whether the subjective experience of time is a fundamental aspect of consciousness.

Overall, the role of time in quantum consciousness is still a topic of active research and debate. While quantum mechanics has provided new insights into the nature of time, it has also raised new questions and challenges to our traditional understanding of time and its relation to consciousness. Further research in this area may provide a deeper understanding of the interplay between time, consciousness, and the quantum world.

One possible avenue for further exploration is the investigation of the relationship between time and memory. The nature of memory and its relation to time is a long-standing question in neuroscience and psychology, and quantum mechanics may offer new insights into this phenomenon. For example, the concept of quantum entanglement suggests that information may be stored and retrieved in a non-local way, meaning that memories may not be strictly bound to specific points in time but may exist in a multi-dimensional space. Additionally, the subjective nature of time in quantum consciousness may provide a new framework for understanding the role of memory in shaping our perception of time.

Another area of exploration is the relationship between time, consciousness, and the emergence of complex systems. The concept of emergence suggests that complex systems can arise from the interactions of simple components, and this may have implications for the nature of time and consciousness. For example, the emergence of consciousness may be related to the complex interactions between neurons in the brain, and the subjective experience of time may emerge from the interactions between the different components of consciousness.

Overall, the study of time in quantum consciousness offers a rich and exciting area for exploration and discovery. As we continue to deepen our understanding of the quantum world, we may gain new insights into the nature of time and its relationship to consciousness, memory, and the emergence of complex systems.

CHAPTER 17.3: CRITICISMS OF THE CONNECTION BETWEEN QUANTUM MECHANICS AND THE CONCEPT OF TIME

The connection between quantum mechanics and the concept of time has been a subject of debate among physicists and philosophers for decades. While some researchers have proposed that quantum mechanics offers a new understanding of time, others have criticized the connection between the two concepts.

One criticism of the connection between quantum mechanics and the concept of time is that it remains unclear how the theory can be applied to the macroscopic world. While quantum mechanics has been successful in explaining phenomena at the atomic and subatomic levels, it has yet to be fully integrated into our understanding of the classical world. As such, the concept of time in quantum mechanics may be limited to the microscopic level, and may not have any bearing on our everyday experience of time.

Another criticism of the connection between quantum mechanics and the concept of time is that it is still unclear how consciousness fits into the picture. While some researchers have proposed that consciousness may play a role in the collapse of the wave function and the measurement problem, it remains unclear how exactly consciousness interacts with the quantum world. Some critics have argued that the connection between quantum mechanics and consciousness is speculative and lacks empirical support.

Additionally, some researchers have criticized the notion that the present moment is not an isolated event, but rather is connected to events that have occurred in the past and will occur in the future. They argue that this view is based on a misinterpretation of entanglement and the non-locality of quantum mechanics. While entanglement suggests that particles can be correlated regardless of distance, it does not necessarily imply a connection between events in time. As such, the connection between quantum mechanics and the concept of time may be overstated and in need of further investigation.

Another criticism of the connection between quantum mechanics and the concept of time is that it does not offer a complete explanation of the arrow of time. The arrow of time refers to the observation that certain processes, such as the flow of heat from hot to cold objects, only occur in one direction. While quantum mechanics may provide insights into the behavior of particles at the microscopic level, it has yet to fully explain why time appears to only move in one direction at the macroscopic level.

Despite these criticisms, the connection between quantum mechanics and the concept of time remains an active area of research and debate. Many researchers continue to explore the potential implications of quantum mechanics on our understanding of time and the nature of reality. Some have proposed that the connection between the two concepts may offer a new perspective on the nature of causality, determinism, and free will.

Furthermore, the study of quantum consciousness may shed new light on the connection between quantum mechanics and the concept of time. By investigating the role of consciousness in the collapse of the wave function and the measurement problem, researchers may gain a deeper understanding of the nature of time and its relationship to the quantum world. Additionally, the study of quantum consciousness may offer insights into the relationship between subjective experience and objective reality, and may help us to better understand the nature of consciousness itself.

In conclusion, the connection between quantum mechanics and the concept of time remains a subject of intense debate and investigation. While some researchers have proposed that quantum mechanics offers a new understanding of time, others have criticized the connection between the two concepts. Despite these criticisms, the study of quantum consciousness may provide new insights into the relationship between quantum mechanics and the concept of time, and may offer a deeper understanding of the nature of reality and consciousness itself.

CHAPTER 18: QUANTUM CONSCIOUSNESS AND THE AFTERLIFE

The concept of an afterlife has been a subject of fascination and speculation for centuries. Many religions and belief systems propose the idea that consciousness persists beyond physical death, and the nature of the afterlife has been a topic of debate and discussion for centuries. In recent years, the connection between quantum consciousness and the afterlife has become an area of interest for some researchers and thinkers.

The idea that quantum mechanics may hold the key to understanding the afterlife is based on the concept of entanglement, which suggests that particles can become connected in a way that transcends space and time. Some proponents of the connection between quantum consciousness and the afterlife suggest that consciousness may be entangled with the fabric of the universe in a similar way, allowing for the possibility of consciousness existing beyond the physical body.

One possible explanation for the persistence of consciousness beyond death is based on the idea of non-locality, which suggests that particles can communicate instantaneously, regardless of the distance between them. This means that consciousness, which is thought to be a non-physical entity, may be able to exist beyond the physical body and communicate with other non-local consciousness.

Another potential link between quantum consciousness and the afterlife is based on the concept of superposition, which suggests that particles can exist in multiple states simultaneously. Some proponents of the afterlife suggest that consciousness may exist in a similar state of superposition, existing in multiple states simultaneously and potentially continuing to exist in some form after the physical body has died.

However, it's important to note that these ideas are highly speculative and have not been scientifically proven. The concept of an afterlife is based on religious and philosophical beliefs, and while some theories may draw on the concepts of quantum mechanics, they remain speculative and unproven.

Furthermore, the concept of an afterlife raises many philosophical and ethical questions. If consciousness can persist beyond the physical body, what form does it take? Is it the same as the consciousness experienced during life, or does it take on a different form? If consciousness does continue to exist beyond death, what is the purpose or function of this existence?

These questions highlight the limitations of our current understanding of consciousness and the afterlife. While the concepts of quantum mechanics may provide some insight into the nature of consciousness, they are not yet able to fully explain the complex and multifaceted concept of an afterlife.

In addition, the concept of an afterlife is often intertwined with cultural and religious beliefs, and interpretations of the afterlife can vary widely between different belief systems. While some may find comfort in the idea of an afterlife, others may find it troubling or even threatening to their worldview.

It's also important to note that the scientific study of consciousness is still in its early stages, and much is still unknown about the nature of consciousness and how it relates to the physical world. While the concepts of quantum mechanics may provide some insight, they are not yet able to fully explain the complex nature of consciousness and its potential relationship to the afterlife.

In conclusion, the connection between quantum consciousness and the afterlife remains a highly speculative area of study. While the concepts of quantum mechanics may provide some insight into the nature of consciousness, they are not yet able to fully explain the complex and multifaceted concept of an afterlife. The idea of an afterlife is often intertwined with cultural and religious beliefs, and interpretations of the afterlife can vary widely between different belief systems. The scientific study of consciousness is still in its early stages, and much is still unknown about the nature of consciousness and its potential relationship to the afterlife.

CHAPTER 18.1: THE CONNECTION BETWEEN QUANTUM CONSCIOUSNESS AND THE AFTERLIFE

The concept of the afterlife has been a topic of discussion and speculation for centuries. While some believe in an afterlife, others are skeptical or do not believe in it at all. However, the idea of the afterlife has taken on a new dimension with the emergence of quantum mechanics and quantum consciousness.

Quantum mechanics suggests that the universe operates in a non-deterministic way, meaning that events can occur without a predetermined cause. It also suggests that particles can exist in multiple states simultaneously, and that these states can be influenced by the act of observation. These principles have led some researchers to suggest that quantum consciousness may play a role in the afterlife.

One theory is that consciousness exists beyond the physical body, and that it may be possible for consciousness to exist after death. This idea is based on the concept of entanglement, which suggests that particles can become entangled and remain connected even when separated by great distances. Some researchers have proposed that consciousness may also be able to become entangled with other forms of consciousness, and that this entanglement could persist even after death.

This theory is supported by the work of physicist Roger Penrose, who has suggested that consciousness may be rooted in quantum mechanics. Penrose has proposed that consciousness arises from quantum processes that occur in microtubules, which are tiny structures found in cells. He suggests that these quantum processes are responsible for the complex computations that occur in the brain, and that they may also be responsible for the subjective experience of consciousness.

If consciousness is indeed rooted in quantum mechanics, it is possible that it may continue to exist after death. Some researchers have suggested that the collapse of the wave function at the moment of death could create a portal that allows consciousness to move beyond the physical body and into a new realm. This new realm could be an afterlife, or it could be a different plane of existence altogether.

Another theory is that consciousness may exist in a higher-dimensional space that is not bound by the laws of time and space. This idea is based on the work of physicist David Bohm, who proposed that there may be hidden dimensions that we are not aware of. He suggested that these hidden dimensions may be responsible for the non-locality and entanglement that we observe in quantum mechanics.

If consciousness exists in a higher-dimensional space, it may be possible for it to continue to exist after death. This idea is supported by the work of near-death experience (NDE) researchers, who have documented cases of people experiencing a sense of leaving their physical bodies and entering into a different realm of existence. While the scientific validity of NDEs is still a matter of debate, these experiences provide anecdotal evidence for the possibility of an afterlife.

It is important to note that the idea of an afterlife rooted in quantum consciousness is still highly speculative and controversial. While some researchers have suggested that quantum mechanics may play a role in the afterlife, there is no concrete evidence to support this idea. The scientific study of consciousness and the afterlife is still in its infancy, and much more research is needed to understand the relationship between quantum mechanics and the concept of an afterlife.

Furthermore, the idea of an afterlife raises important ethical and moral questions. If consciousness does indeed continue to exist after death, what happens to the individual's identity, memories, and personality? Is it possible for consciousness to exist without these elements? How does this relate to traditional religious beliefs about the afterlife? These are complex questions that require careful consideration and investigation.

In conclusion, the connection between quantum consciousness and the afterlife is an area of ongoing speculation and investigation. While some researchers have suggested that quantum mechanics may play a role in the afterlife, there is currently no concrete evidence to

CHAPTER 18.2: THE IMPLICATIONS OF QUANTUM CONSCIOUSNESS FOR LIFE AFTER DEATH

The connection between quantum consciousness and the afterlife has been a topic of much speculation and debate. While there is no scientific evidence to support the idea of an afterlife, some researchers have proposed that quantum mechanics may offer a possible mechanism for the continuation of consciousness after death.

One of the key ideas behind this proposal is the concept of entanglement, which suggests that particles can become entangled in a way that allows them to remain connected even when separated by great distances. This phenomenon has led some to speculate that consciousness may also be entangled with the universe in a way that allows it to persist after death.

One proposed mechanism for the continuation of consciousness after death is through a process known as quantum tunneling. This process involves the transfer of information from one particle to another through a barrier that would normally be impenetrable. Some researchers have suggested that this process may allow consciousness to continue beyond the physical body, by transferring information from the brain to a non-physical medium, such as a quantum field.

Another proposed mechanism is through the concept of the

holographic universe. This theory suggests that the universe is a hologram, in which all information is encoded on a two-dimensional surface. Some researchers have proposed that consciousness may also be a hologram, with all of our experiences and memories encoded on a two-dimensional surface. If this is true, then it may be possible for consciousness to continue after death, by transferring this holographic information to another dimension.

While these proposals are speculative, they highlight the potential implications of quantum consciousness for the concept of life after death. If consciousness is indeed entangled with the universe in a way that allows it to persist beyond the physical body, then it may be possible that our consciousness continues on after death, in some form or another.

However, these proposals also raise a number of questions and challenges. For example, if consciousness does continue after death, then what form does it take? Does it retain the same personality, memories, and sense of self that it had in life, or is it something entirely different? And if consciousness does continue after death, then what is the purpose or function of this continuation? Is it simply an artifact of the laws of physics, or does it serve some greater purpose or meaning?

These questions are difficult to answer, and may ultimately be impossible to answer with our current understanding of the universe. However, they highlight the need for continued research into the relationship between quantum mechanics and consciousness, and the potential implications of this relationship for our understanding of life and death.

In addition to the scientific and philosophical implications of quantum consciousness for life after death, there are also a number of ethical and cultural implications. For example, if consciousness does continue after death, then this may have implications for end-of-life care and the treatment of the dying. It may also challenge traditional beliefs about death and the afterlife, and raise new questions about the purpose and meaning of life.

Furthermore, the idea of an afterlife based on quantum consciousness may have cultural and religious implications, particularly for those who believe in a traditional afterlife. It may challenge these beliefs, and raise questions about the nature of the afterlife and the role of consciousness in it.

Overall, the implications of quantum consciousness for life after death are complex and far-reaching. While there is currently no scientific evidence to support the idea of an afterlife, the concept of entanglement and other principles of quantum mechanics offer intriguing possibilities for the continuation of consciousness beyond the physical body. These possibilities raise important questions and challenges, both scientific and philosophical, and highlight the need for continued research and exploration into the relationship between quantum mechanics and consciousness.

CHAPTER 18.3: CRITICISMS OF THE CONNECTION BETWEEN QUANTUM CONSCIOUSNESS AND THE AFTERLIFE

The idea that quantum consciousness could be linked to the afterlife is a controversial one, and there are several criticisms of this connection.

One of the main criticisms is that there is no scientific evidence to support the existence of an afterlife. While there have been numerous reports of near-death experiences, past life memories, and encounters with deceased loved ones, these phenomena are difficult to verify and replicate in a scientific setting. Without empirical evidence, it is difficult to draw any definitive conclusions about the nature of the afterlife.

Furthermore, some skeptics argue that the connection between quantum mechanics and the afterlife is simply an attempt to use scientific jargon to give credibility to mystical or religious beliefs. They argue that the concepts of quantum mechanics are often misunderstood or misused by individuals seeking to validate their pre-existing beliefs, and that the afterlife is simply another example of this.

Another criticism is that the idea of a quantum afterlife is too vague and speculative to be of any real use. Even if it were possible to establish a connection between quantum mechanics and consciousness, it is unclear how this would translate into an afterlife. Would consciousness continue to exist in a different form, or would it simply cease to exist altogether? Without a clear understanding of what the afterlife might look like, it is difficult to say how quantum mechanics might be involved.

Finally, some critics argue that the concept of an afterlife is inherently problematic from a philosophical standpoint. If consciousness can exist independently of the body, then what is the nature of this consciousness? Is it a separate entity that can exist outside of time and space, or is it simply a product of the physical brain? And if consciousness does continue to exist after death, then what is the purpose of life on Earth? These are deep and complex questions that may never be fully answered.

In conclusion, while the idea of a quantum afterlife is intriguing, it remains a speculative and controversial topic. While there are some tantalizing connections between quantum mechanics and consciousness, there is currently no empirical evidence to support the existence of an afterlife. As such, any claims about the nature of the afterlife must be viewed with a healthy degree of skepticism and caution.

CHAPTER 19: THE FUTURE OF QUANTUM CONSCIOUSNESS RESEARCH

The study of quantum consciousness is still in its infancy, and much research needs to be done before we can fully understand the nature of consciousness and its connection to quantum mechanics. However, the current state of research provides some clues as to the future direction of this field.

One of the most promising areas of research is the study of entanglement and its connection to consciousness. As we have seen, entanglement suggests that consciousness is not an isolated phenomenon, but is connected to the rest of the universe in a fundamental way. The study of entanglement can therefore provide insights into the nature of consciousness and its relationship to the physical world.

Another area of research that holds promise is the study of quantum information processing in the brain. As we have seen, the brain appears to be able to process information in a way that is similar to quantum computers. This suggests that quantum computing techniques may be useful in understanding the workings of the brain and consciousness.

In addition, research into the connection between quantum mechanics and the concept of time may also yield important insights into the nature of consciousness. The study of entanglement suggests that the present moment is not isolated, but is connected to events that have occurred in the past and will occur in the future. This suggests that our experience of time may be more complex than we currently understand, and that quantum mechanics may provide a new framework for understanding this phenomenon.

However, there are also significant challenges facing researchers in the field of quantum consciousness. One of the major challenges is the difficulty of conducting experiments that can definitively demonstrate the connection between quantum mechanics and consciousness. Many of the experiments that have been conducted thus far are subject to criticism and debate, and more work needs to be done to develop more robust experimental techniques.

In addition, there is also the challenge of developing a theoretical framework for understanding the connection between quantum mechanics and consciousness. While there are many theories and hypotheses in this field, there is no consensus on a single theory that can fully explain the phenomenon of consciousness in terms of quantum mechanics.

Despite these challenges, there is reason to be optimistic about the future of quantum consciousness research. As our understanding of quantum mechanics continues to evolve, we may be able to develop new experimental techniques and theoretical frameworks that can shed light on the nature of consciousness and its relationship to the physical world.

One promising area of research is the study of the brain at the molecular level. Advances in molecular biology and neurochemistry may allow researchers to study the quantum properties of individual neurons and molecules within the brain, providing new insights into the workings of the brain and consciousness.

Another area of research that may yield important insights into quantum consciousness is the study of the microbiome – the collection of microorganisms that live within our bodies. Recent research has suggested that the microbiome may play a significant role in the functioning of the brain and nervous system. The study of the microbiome and its relationship to consciousness may therefore provide new avenues of research for quantum consciousness researchers.

Finally, advances in artificial intelligence and machine learning may also play a significant role in the future of quantum consciousness research. As we continue to develop more powerful computing technologies, we may be able to simulate and model the workings of the brain and consciousness in a way that was previously impossible.

In conclusion, the study of quantum consciousness is a rapidly evolving field that holds great promise for our understanding of the nature of consciousness and its relationship to the physical world. While there are significant challenges facing researchers in this field, there are also many reasons to be optimistic about the future of quantum consciousness research. With continued advances in experimental techniques, theoretical frameworks, and computing technologies, we may be able to unlock the secrets of consciousness and its connection to the quantum world in the years to come.

CHAPTER 19.1: THE CURRENT STATE OF QUANTUM CONSCIOUSNESS RESEARCH

Quantum consciousness is a relatively new field of study, and much research is still needed to fully understand the nature of the relationship between quantum mechanics and consciousness. Despite this, there have been several significant findings and developments in the field in recent years.

One of the key areas of research in quantum consciousness has been the study of the brain and its connection to quantum mechanics. Many researchers believe that the brain may be a key player in the emergence of consciousness, and that quantum mechanics may play a role in this process. Studies have shown that certain types of neurons in the brain may exhibit quantum behavior, and that quantum entanglement may play a role in the functioning of neural networks.

Another area of research in quantum consciousness has been the study of the role of quantum mechanics in perception and cognition. Some researchers have suggested that the act of perception itself may involve a collapse of the wave function, and that this collapse may be related to the emergence of conscious experience. Other researchers have focused on the role of quantum mechanics in the processing and storage of information, and how this may be related to the functioning of the brain and the emergence of consciousness.

One of the challenges in quantum consciousness research

is the difficulty of designing experiments that can test the relationship between quantum mechanics and consciousness. Many of the phenomena that are believed to be related to quantum consciousness, such as the collapse of the wave function, are difficult to observe directly, and may only be inferred from other experimental results. This has led some researchers to develop new experimental techniques, such as the use of quantum sensors and quantum computers, to study the behavior of quantum systems in the context of consciousness.

Despite these challenges, there have been several significant breakthroughs in quantum consciousness research in recent years. One such breakthrough was the discovery of quantum vibrations in microtubules in neurons, which may play a role in the processing and storage of information in the brain. Another significant development was the demonstration of quantum entanglement between photons in the brains of two individuals, which suggests that quantum mechanics may play a role in social interactions and communication.

Overall, the current state of quantum consciousness research is still in its infancy, but there is growing interest and excitement in the field. As more researchers become involved in the study of quantum mechanics and consciousness, it is likely that new discoveries will be made that will shed light on the nature of consciousness and its relationship to the quantum world.

In the next section, we will discuss some of the future directions of quantum consciousness research, and the potential challenges of these developments for our understanding of the mind and the nature of reality.

CHAPTER 19.2: THE CHALLENGES FACING QUANTUM CONSCIOUSNESS RESEARCH

Quantum consciousness is a field of study that is still in its infancy. While there has been significant progress in understanding the connection between quantum mechanics and consciousness, there are still many challenges facing researchers in this area. In this chapter, we will explore some of the challenges facing quantum consciousness research.

One of the major challenges facing quantum consciousness research is the lack of experimental evidence. While there have been a number of experiments that suggest a connection between quantum mechanics and consciousness, these experiments are still controversial and there is a lack of consensus among scientists. In addition, many of these experiments are difficult to replicate and there are often conflicting results. This lack of experimental evidence makes it difficult to establish a clear connection between quantum mechanics and consciousness.

Another challenge facing quantum consciousness research is the lack of a clear definition of consciousness. While there are many theories about what consciousness is and how it works, there is no widely accepted definition of consciousness. This lack of consensus makes it difficult to design experiments that can accurately measure consciousness and its relationship to quantum mechanics.

Another challenge is the complexity of the brain. The brain is an incredibly complex organ, and understanding how it works is one of the biggest challenges facing neuroscience. While there have been significant advances in brain imaging and other techniques, there is still much that is not understood about the brain. This complexity makes it difficult to study the connection between quantum mechanics and consciousness in a systematic way.

In addition to these challenges, there are also philosophical challenges facing quantum consciousness research. One of the major challenges is the problem of dualism. Dualism is the idea that consciousness is a separate entity from the physical world, and that it cannot be explained solely by physical processes. This idea is at odds with the principles of quantum mechanics, which suggest that everything in the universe is interconnected and that there is no separation between the physical world and consciousness. This philosophical challenge makes it difficult to reconcile the principles of quantum mechanics with our intuitive understanding of consciousness.

Another philosophical challenge is the problem of reductionism. Reductionism is the idea that complex phenomena can be explained by reducing them to their simplest components. While reductionism has been a powerful tool in many areas of science, it is not clear whether it can fully explain consciousness. Consciousness is a complex and multifaceted phenomenon, and it is not clear whether it can be fully understood by reducing it to its simplest components.

Despite these challenges, there is still much optimism about the future of quantum consciousness research. Advances in technology, such as brain imaging techniques and quantum computers, may allow researchers to better understand the connection between quantum mechanics and consciousness. In addition, there is a growing community of researchers who are dedicated to studying quantum consciousness, and who are working to develop new experimental and theoretical approaches to this field.

One promising area of research is the study of entanglement in the brain. As we discussed earlier, entanglement is a phenomenon in which two particles become connected in such a way that the state of one particle is dependent on the state of the other, even when they are separated by large distances. Some researchers have suggested that entanglement may play a role in consciousness, and that the brain may use entanglement to process information in a way that is different from classical computers.

Another promising area of research is the study of quantum coherence in the brain. Quantum coherence is a phenomenon in which particles become synchronized in such a way that they act as a single entity. Some researchers have suggested that quantum coherence may play a role in consciousness, and that the brain may use coherence to process information in a way that is different from classical computers.

In addition to these areas of research, there is also a growing interest in the philosophical implications of quantum consciousness. Some philosophers have suggested that the principles of quantum mechanics may have implications for the nature of reality, the existence of free will, and the relationship between mind and matter. For example, some have argued that the observer effect and entanglement imply a fundamental interconnectedness between all things in the universe, blurring the traditional boundaries between the observer and the observed.

Another area of philosophical inquiry is the relationship between consciousness and the physical world. Some have proposed that consciousness is not simply a byproduct of brain activity, but rather a fundamental aspect of the universe. They argue that just as matter and energy are two sides of the same coin, consciousness and physical reality may also be two aspects of a single underlying reality.

Despite the many challenges facing quantum consciousness research, the potential implications for our understanding of consciousness and the universe are too significant to ignore. With advances in technology and a growing interest in the field, it is likely that we will continue to make progress in this area of research in the coming years. As we do, we may gain a deeper appreciation for the mysteries of consciousness and the interconnectedness of all things in the universe.

CHAPTER 19.3: THE PROMISING AREAS FOR FUTURE QUANTUM CONSCIOUSNESS RESEARCH

Despite the challenges facing quantum consciousness research, there are several promising areas for future investigation that could provide valuable insights into the nature of consciousness and its relationship with quantum mechanics.

One promising area is the study of non-locality and entanglement in the brain. As discussed earlier, entanglement is a phenomenon in which two particles become correlated in such a way that the state of one particle depends on the state of the other, regardless of the distance between them. Non-locality is the idea that information can be transmitted instantaneously between entangled particles, violating the classical limit of the speed of light. Some researchers have proposed that entanglement may play a role in neural communication, and that the brain may use non-local connections to integrate information from different areas.

Another promising area of research is the study of quantum coherence in biological systems. Coherence refers to the degree to which a system can maintain a stable phase relationship between different parts, and is a key feature of quantum systems. Researchers have found evidence of coherence in biological systems, such as photosynthesis and olfaction, and have suggested that coherence may also be present in neural processes. Understanding the role of coherence in the brain could provide insights into the mechanisms underlying consciousness.

A third area of interest is the study of quantum thermodynamics in the brain. Thermodynamics is the study of the relationship between heat, energy, and work, and is a fundamental concept in physics. Quantum thermodynamics is the study of these same relationships in quantum systems. Researchers have proposed that the brain may use quantum thermodynamic processes to increase energy efficiency and optimize information processing.

Finally, there is growing interest in the study of the role of quantum mechanics in higher-order cognitive processes, such as decision making and introspection. While much of the current research has focused on the relationship between quantum mechanics and basic sensory perception, it is possible that quantum mechanics may also play a role in more complex cognitive processes. Understanding the role of quantum mechanics in these higher-order processes could provide a more comprehensive understanding of the relationship between consciousness and quantum mechanics.

In conclusion, while the study of quantum consciousness is still in its early stages, there are several promising areas of research that could provide valuable insights into the nature of consciousness and its relationship with quantum mechanics. Despite the challenges and criticisms facing the field, the interdisciplinary approach taken by researchers in this area holds great potential for advancing our understanding of one of the greatest mysteries of human existence.

CHAPTER 20: QUANTUM ETHICS

Quantum mechanics has revolutionized our understanding of the fundamental nature of reality. It has also raised important questions about the ethical implications of the new scientific paradigm. In this chapter, we will explore the emerging field of quantum ethics, which seeks to address the ethical questions arising from the insights of quantum mechanics.

The Need for Quantum Ethics

The traditional ethical frameworks that have been used to guide human behavior are based on classical physics and do not fully account for the unique features of quantum mechanics. The principles of quantum mechanics, such as entanglement and superposition, challenge traditional notions of causality and determinism, and raise important ethical questions about the nature of human agency, responsibility, and decision-making.

For example, the concept of entanglement suggests that the actions of one person can affect the outcomes of distant events, even without any direct causal connection. This raises questions about the responsibility of individuals for the unintended consequences of their actions, and the limits of individual agency in a universe where the boundaries of causality are blurred.

Similarly, the principle of superposition suggests that physical systems can exist in multiple states simultaneously, which raises questions about the nature of decision-making and the role of free will. If the universe is fundamentally indeterminate, as some interpretations of quantum mechanics suggest, then how can individuals be held responsible for their choices?

These and other questions highlight the need for a new ethical framework that can account for the insights of quantum mechanics and guide human behavior in an increasingly complex and interconnected world.

The Principles of Quantum Ethics

Quantum ethics is still a nascent field, but several principles have emerged that can guide ethical decision-making in the quantum era.

The first principle is the recognition of the interconnectedness of all things. The principle of entanglement suggests that everything in the universe is connected in some way, and that the actions of one person can have ripple effects throughout the world. This principle calls for a greater sense of responsibility and empathy towards all living beings, and an awareness of the impact of our actions on the larger web of existence.

The second principle is the recognition of the indeterminacy of the universe. The principle of superposition suggests that the universe is fundamentally indeterminate, and that events are not determined by prior causes in a deterministic sense. This principle calls for a greater sense of humility and openness to uncertainty, and a recognition that our choices are not predetermined by past events or external forces.

The third principle is the recognition of the importance of perspective. The principles of quantum mechanics suggest that the observer plays a fundamental role in the measurement and interpretation of physical phenomena. This principle calls for a greater awareness of the subjective nature of our perceptions and the limitations of our knowledge, and a recognition that different perspectives can lead to different ethical conclusions.

The fourth principle is the recognition of the importance of complexity. The principles of quantum mechanics suggest that the universe is inherently complex and interconnected, and that simple cause-and-effect models may not fully capture the nature of reality. This principle calls for a greater appreciation of the complexity of ethical decision-making and a recognition that simple solutions may not always be sufficient to address complex ethical dilemmas.

Applications of Quantum Ethics

The principles of quantum ethics have wide-ranging applications in fields such as environmental ethics, medical ethics, and business ethics.

In environmental ethics, the principle of interconnectedness calls for a greater sense of responsibility towards the natural world, and an awareness of the impact of human actions on the delicate balance of ecosystems. This principle can guide ethical decision-making in areas such as climate change, conservation, and sustainable development.

In medical ethics, the principle of indeterminacy calls for a recognition of the limits of medical knowledge and the importance of patient autonomy. This principle can guide ethical decision-making in areas such as end-of-life care, where the unpredictability of quantum systems could make it impossible to accurately predict a patient's outcome. This highlights the importance of respecting the patient's right to make their own decisions about their care, even if those decisions may result in an uncertain outcome.

Quantum ethics also has implications for environmental ethics, where the interconnectedness of quantum systems can be used to justify the protection of ecosystems and the recognition of the intrinsic value of all living things. The concept of entanglement, in particular, emphasizes the interconnectedness of all things, and highlights the impact that human actions can have on the environment.

In addition, quantum ethics may also have implications for social and political ethics. The concept of superposition, for example, could be used to promote social justice by recognizing that individuals can exist in multiple states at once, and that these states can be influenced by external factors such as discrimination or poverty. By acknowledging the complexity and interconnectedness of social systems, quantum ethics may provide a framework for promoting equality and justice.

However, there are also challenges facing the development of quantum ethics. One of the main challenges is the difficulty in applying quantum principles to ethical decision-making in a practical and consistent manner. The complexity and unpredictability of quantum systems can make it difficult to make accurate predictions about the outcomes of different actions, and this can create uncertainty in ethical decision-making.

Another challenge is the potential for misuse or misinterpretation of quantum principles in ethical contexts. The complexity of quantum systems can make it easy for individuals to selectively interpret quantum principles in a way that supports their own beliefs or interests, rather than in a way that is consistent with the principles of quantum mechanics.

Despite these challenges, the development of quantum ethics

has the potential to provide a new and innovative approach to ethical decision-making. By incorporating the principles of quantum mechanics, quantum ethics may offer a more nuanced and sophisticated understanding of the interconnectedness of all things, and the impact that our actions can have on the world around us. As quantum consciousness research continues to evolve, the development of quantum ethics may become an increasingly important area of study, with implications for a wide range of ethical domains.

CHAPTER 20.1: THE ETHICAL IMPLICATIONS OF QUANTUM CONSCIOUSNESS

The emergence of quantum consciousness has led to new discussions and debates regarding the ethical implications of this field. The potential impact of quantum mechanics on ethical theories and principles has been a topic of interest for philosophers and scientists alike. This chapter aims to explore some of the ethical implications of quantum consciousness and how they may shape our understanding of ethics.

One of the main ethical implications of quantum consciousness is the potential for a new understanding of consciousness itself. If consciousness is not simply a product of the brain but rather an intrinsic part of the fabric of the universe, as some theories suggest, then our ethical considerations may need to expand beyond the human realm. The implications of this idea are vast and may lead to a re-examination of our relationship with other living beings and the environment.

Quantum consciousness also has implications for our understanding of free will and moral responsibility. The uncertainty principle of quantum mechanics suggests that the universe is fundamentally indeterminate and that the actions of subatomic particles are not predetermined. This idea challenges traditional notions of determinism and raises questions about whether individuals have true free will or if their actions are predetermined. The implications of this for moral responsibility are significant, as it may call into question our ability to hold individuals accountable for their actions.

In addition, the concept of entanglement in quantum mechanics may have ethical implications for our relationships with others. Entanglement suggests that individuals are not separate entities but rather interconnected and that our actions can have an impact beyond our immediate surroundings. This idea challenges the traditional Western view of individualism and may lead to a greater emphasis on collective responsibility.

Quantum mechanics also challenges traditional ethical theories such as consequentialism and deontology. Consequentialism holds that the morality of an action is determined by its outcome, while deontology holds that the morality of an action is determined by its adherence to moral rules. The uncertainty principle of quantum mechanics suggests that outcomes cannot be predicted with certainty, which challenges the foundations of consequentialism. Similarly, the indeterminate nature of quantum mechanics challenges the strict rules of deontology.

Furthermore, the concept of superposition in quantum mechanics may have implications for our understanding of moral decision-making. Superposition suggests that particles can exist in multiple states simultaneously until they are observed or measured. This idea challenges traditional notions of objectivity and suggests that subjective experience plays a role in determining reality. This may have implications for ethical decision-making, as it may call into question the objectivity of moral principles.

The implications of quantum mechanics for the ethics of science and technology are also significant. The uncertainty principle and the indeterminate nature of quantum mechanics suggest that science cannot provide definitive answers and that there are limits to our knowledge. This may call for a greater emphasis on caution and humility in scientific research and a recognition of the potential risks and unintended consequences of technological advancements.

Finally, the potential for quantum computing to revolutionize data processing raises ethical concerns regarding privacy and security. The ability of quantum computers to perform calculations exponentially faster than classical computers may allow for the decryption of encrypted data and the circumvention of traditional security measures. This may have significant implications for personal privacy and national security.

In conclusion, quantum consciousness has far-reaching ethical implications that challenge traditional ethical theories and principles. The potential impact of quantum mechanics on our understanding of consciousness, free will, moral responsibility, and ethical decision-making may lead to a re-examination of our relationship with other living beings, the environment, and technology. It is important that we continue to explore these ethical implications as quantum consciousness research continues to evolve.

CHAPTER 20.2: THE ROLE OF ETHICS IN QUANTUM CONSCIOUSNESS STUDIES

As the study of quantum consciousness advances, it is important to consider the role of ethics in research and application of this field. Ethics involves the moral principles and values that guide individual and collective behavior, and it is essential in ensuring that scientific research is conducted in a responsible and just manner.

One of the main ethical concerns in quantum consciousness research is the potential for misuse of knowledge and technology. For example, the ability to manipulate quantum states of matter and energy could lead to the development of powerful new technologies with both beneficial and harmful applications. Therefore, it is crucial that researchers take into account the potential social and environmental impacts of their work and consider the possible ethical implications of their findings.

Another ethical issue in quantum consciousness research relates to the treatment of sentient beings. While many researchers focus on the study of non-human consciousness, it is essential to consider the ethical implications of any research that involves the manipulation or modification of conscious beings, including animals and humans. In particular, ethical considerations should be taken into account when developing new treatments or therapies based on quantum principles.

Furthermore, the study of consciousness raises important

questions about the nature of personal identity, autonomy, and privacy. As we gain a deeper understanding of the mechanisms underlying consciousness, we may be able to manipulate and even control the thoughts, feelings, and actions of others. This raises serious ethical questions about the extent to which individuals should be allowed to manipulate the consciousness of others and the potential consequences of doing so.

The principles of informed consent and privacy are essential in ensuring that research involving human subjects is conducted in an ethical manner. Researchers must obtain informed consent from participants, meaning that participants fully understand the nature and purpose of the research and voluntarily agree to participate. Additionally, researchers must ensure that participant confidentiality is maintained, protecting their personal information and data from unauthorized access or disclosure.

Moreover, quantum ethics also involves consideration of the potential impact of research on future generations. The development of new technologies and knowledge may have long-term effects that are not fully understood, and researchers must consider the potential risks and benefits of their work for future generations.

In addition to these ethical concerns, the interdisciplinary nature of quantum consciousness research raises challenges in terms of collaboration and communication between scientists from different disciplines. As quantum consciousness research involves both physics and neuroscience, researchers from these fields may have different perspectives on ethical issues related to their work. It is essential that these differences are acknowledged and that a collaborative and multidisciplinary approach is adopted to address ethical concerns in quantum consciousness research.

To address these ethical issues, the field of quantum ethics has emerged. Quantum ethics is a branch of ethics that explores the ethical implications of quantum mechanics and quantum technologies. This field involves collaboration between scientists, philosophers, and ethicists, and aims to develop ethical frameworks that can guide the responsible use of quantum technologies and knowledge.

In conclusion, ethics plays a crucial role in quantum consciousness research, guiding researchers to conduct their work in a responsible and just manner. Ethical concerns related to the potential misuse of knowledge and technology, treatment of sentient beings, personal identity and autonomy, informed consent and privacy, and the impact on future generations must be considered. The emerging field of quantum ethics aims to address these concerns and develop ethical frameworks for the responsible use of quantum technologies and knowledge.

CHAPTER 20.3: THE NEED FOR RESPONSIBLE RESEARCH IN QUANTUM CONSCIOUSNESS

As the field of quantum consciousness continues to develop, it is important to consider the ethical implications of research in this area. While there is great potential for new insights and discoveries, there are also risks associated with new technology and knowledge. Responsible research practices can help to ensure that the benefits of quantum consciousness are maximized while minimizing any potential negative consequences.

One of the primary concerns related to quantum consciousness research is the potential for misuse of information or technology. For example, if researchers were to discover a way to manipulate consciousness through quantum technology, this could have significant implications for personal privacy, security, and autonomy. There is also the potential for new forms of discrimination or bias if certain groups have greater access to or control over quantum consciousness technologies.

To address these concerns, it is important for researchers to consider the ethical implications of their work from the outset. This means considering the potential impacts on individuals, communities, and society as a whole, and taking steps to mitigate any negative consequences. This might involve working with ethicists, policymakers, and other stakeholders to develop guidelines for responsible research and innovation in the field of quantum consciousness.

One key area of focus for responsible research in quantum consciousness is the development of safeguards to protect personal privacy and autonomy. This might involve developing secure and transparent methods for collecting and storing data related to quantum consciousness, as well as ensuring that individuals have control over how their personal information is used. It might also involve establishing guidelines for the use of quantum consciousness technologies in clinical settings, to ensure that patients are fully informed and have the ability to make informed decisions about their treatment.

Another area of concern is the potential for unintended consequences of quantum consciousness research. For example, researchers might discover a way to manipulate consciousness in a way that has unintended negative effects on mental health or cognitive function. To mitigate these risks, it is important for researchers to conduct rigorous safety and efficacy testing before introducing new technologies or techniques into clinical settings.

In addition to these concerns, there is also a need to consider the broader societal implications of quantum consciousness research. For example, the development of new technologies could have significant impacts on employment, economics, and social structures. It is important for researchers to work with policymakers and other stakeholders to develop strategies for managing these changes and ensuring that the benefits of quantum consciousness are shared fairly and equitably.

Finally, there is a need for transparency and accountability in quantum consciousness research. This means ensuring that researchers are open and honest about their methods and findings, and that they are willing to engage in dialogue with other stakeholders about the potential impacts of their work. It also means ensuring that researchers are willing to take responsibility for any unintended negative consequences of their research, and to work collaboratively with others to address these issues.

In summary, the field of quantum consciousness offers tremendous potential for new insights and discoveries about the nature of consciousness and the universe. However, this potential must be balanced against the need for responsible research and innovation that takes into account the ethical implications of new knowledge and technology. By working collaboratively with ethicists, policymakers, and other stakeholders, researchers can ensure that the benefits of quantum consciousness are realized while minimizing any potential negative consequences. Ultimately, this will help to ensure that the field of quantum consciousness remains a force for good in the world, and that it continues to push the boundaries of our understanding of the universe and our place within it.

CHAPTER 21: CONCLUSION

The study of quantum consciousness is still in its infancy, but it has already had a significant impact on our understanding of consciousness and the world around us. Quantum mechanics has challenged our traditional views of reality and has provided a new framework for understanding the nature of consciousness.

The observer effect, entanglement, and superposition are just a few of the quantum phenomena that have been explored in relation to consciousness. These concepts have challenged the traditional view of the mind-body problem and have opened up new avenues of research into the nature of consciousness.

While there is still much to be discovered in this field, quantum consciousness research has already provided insights into the connections between consciousness and the physical world. It has also raised important ethical questions regarding the responsible use of technology and the potential consequences of our actions.

One of the most intriguing implications of quantum consciousness is its potential to shed light on the nature of subjective experience. By providing a new framework for understanding the mind-body problem, quantum mechanics has the potential to unlock some of the mysteries of consciousness.

Another exciting area of research in quantum consciousness is the study of altered states of consciousness. By examining the effects of psychedelic substances on the brain, researchers are gaining insights into the neural correlates of consciousness and the ways in which consciousness can be altered.

Despite the many exciting possibilities presented by quantum consciousness research, there are also significant challenges that must be addressed. The complexity of the subject matter requires interdisciplinary collaboration and a careful balancing of the risks and benefits of research.

Additionally, as with any new field of research, there are many unknowns and potential pitfalls. The potential consequences of tinkering with the fundamental nature of reality and consciousness are unknown, and it is important that we proceed with caution and ethical considerations.

In conclusion, quantum consciousness is a rapidly evolving field of research that has the potential to revolutionize our understanding of consciousness and the world around us. Its implications for philosophy, psychology, neuroscience, and other fields are vast and exciting. However, it is crucial that we proceed with caution and responsibility, taking into account the ethical considerations of our research and its potential consequences.

As we continue to explore the mysteries of the quantum world and the nature of consciousness, we must remain open to new possibilities and keep an open mind to the potential implications of our findings. Only by working together and embracing the complexity of this subject can we hope to unlock the secrets of the universe and the human mind.

CHAPTER 21.1: THE MAJOR FINDINGS OF QUANTUM CONSCIOUSNESS STUDIES

Throughout this book, we have explored the fascinating world of quantum consciousness and the implications it may have for our understanding of consciousness, reality, and the universe as a whole. In this final chapter, we will summarize the major findings of quantum consciousness studies and their potential impact on science, philosophy, and society.

One of the key findings of quantum consciousness research is that the brain may operate at the quantum level. While traditional neuroscience has focused on the classical mechanics of neurons and synapses, recent research has suggested that quantum phenomena, such as entanglement and superposition, may also play a role in the brain's functioning. This has led to the development of new theories, such as the Orch-OR theory, which suggest that quantum processes in microtubules within neurons are responsible for consciousness.

Another major finding is the concept of nonlocality, which challenges our traditional understanding of causality and the limits of space and time. Quantum entanglement has been demonstrated to occur between particles separated by vast distances, indicating that they are somehow connected at a fundamental level. This has led to the proposal that consciousness itself may be nonlocal, meaning that it is not limited to the physical boundaries of the brain or body.

The concept of observer effect and the role of consciousness in the collapse of the wave function has also been a major area of study. While this remains a highly debated topic, the idea that the act of observation by a conscious observer can affect the behavior of subatomic particles has significant implications for our understanding of reality and the nature of consciousness itself.

Furthermore, quantum consciousness research has opened up new avenues for exploring the nature of reality and the relationship between mind and matter. The idea that consciousness may play a fundamental role in the creation and organization of the universe challenges traditional scientific and philosophical beliefs. This has led to the development of new models, such as the Participatory Universe, which suggest that consciousness is not merely a byproduct of physical processes but rather a fundamental aspect of the universe.

Overall, quantum consciousness studies have led to a radical rethinking of our understanding of consciousness, reality, and the universe. The implications of these findings are far-reaching, with potential impacts on fields such as neuroscience, physics, philosophy, and spirituality. While many questions remain unanswered and much research is still needed, the study of quantum consciousness has provided us with new insights and perspectives on the nature of our existence.

One of the key challenges facing future research in this area is the need for interdisciplinary collaboration. Quantum consciousness studies require expertise from multiple fields, including physics, neuroscience, philosophy, and psychology. Collaborative efforts will be essential for developing a comprehensive understanding of this complex and fascinating topic.

Another challenge is the need for responsible research practices. The potential implications of quantum consciousness studies are profound, and it is important that research is conducted in an ethical and responsible manner. This includes consideration of the potential impacts of research on society, as well as the importance of transparency and open communication with the public.

In conclusion, the study of quantum consciousness has provided us with a deeper understanding of the nature of reality and the role of consciousness in the universe. The implications of these findings are significant, with potential impacts on fields ranging from neuroscience to spirituality. While much research is still needed, the study of quantum consciousness is an exciting and rapidly developing area that promises to transform our understanding of the universe and our place within it.

CHAPTER 21.2: THE IMPLICATIONS OF QUANTUM CONSCIOUSNESS FOR PHILOSOPHY, SCIENCE, AND SOCIETY

The study of quantum consciousness has profound implications for various fields such as philosophy, science, and society. This chapter will explore the implications of quantum consciousness research for these fields.

Philosophy Quantum consciousness research has challenged the traditional Cartesian view of the mind-body duality. The findings of quantum consciousness suggest that consciousness is not a separate entity from the physical world, but rather an integral part of it. This view aligns with the Eastern philosophy of non-dualism, which suggests that everything in the universe is interconnected.

Furthermore, quantum consciousness research has implications for the philosophy of free will. If the universe is indeterminate at the quantum level, then it raises questions about the concept of free will. Do we have free will, or are our actions predetermined by the laws of nature? This question is still being debated, but quantum consciousness research suggests that our actions may not be predetermined, and we may have more agency than previously thought.

Science Quantum consciousness research has also challenged our understanding of the brain and its functions. Traditionally, the brain was viewed as a deterministic machine, but the findings of quantum mechanics suggest that the brain may not operate in a purely deterministic manner. This has implications for fields such as neuroscience, psychology, and artificial intelligence.

In neuroscience, the findings of quantum consciousness research suggest that the brain may operate on a quantum level, which could explain the non-locality of consciousness. Furthermore, the concept of entanglement suggests that different regions of the brain may be interconnected, which could explain how the brain processes information and generates consciousness.

In psychology, the findings of quantum consciousness research have implications for the study of perception and cognition. For example, the concept of superposition suggests that our perceptions may be influenced by our expectations and beliefs, which could explain the placebo effect.

In artificial intelligence, the findings of quantum consciousness research could lead to the development of quantum computers, which could perform certain computations faster than classical computers. This could have significant implications for fields such as cryptography, finance, and medicine.

Society Finally, quantum consciousness research has implications for society as a whole. The findings of quantum consciousness challenge our understanding of reality and our place in the universe. The concept of non-locality suggests that everything in the universe is interconnected, which could lead to a greater sense of empathy and interconnectedness among people.

Furthermore, the findings of quantum consciousness research have implications for the way we view the environment. If everything in the universe is interconnected, then our actions could have far-reaching consequences. This could lead to a greater sense of responsibility for the environment and a move towards more sustainable living practices.

Conclusion In conclusion, the study of quantum consciousness has profound implications for various fields such as philosophy, science, and society. The findings of quantum consciousness challenge our traditional views of the mind-body duality and our understanding of the brain and its functions. Furthermore, the concept of non-locality suggests that everything in the universe is interconnected, which could lead to a greater sense of empathy and responsibility for the environment. Quantum consciousness research is still in its early stages, and there is much to be discovered about the nature of consciousness and its relationship to the physical world. However, the implications of this research are far-reaching and could lead to significant changes in the way we view ourselves and our place in the universe.

CHAPTER 21.3: THE FUTURE DIRECTIONS OF QUANTUM CONSCIOUSNESS RESEARCH

Quantum consciousness research has made significant progress in the last few decades. However, there is still much to be discovered, and many unanswered questions remain. As quantum mechanics continues to expand our understanding of the universe, it also sheds light on the mysteries of consciousness. In this chapter, we will explore some of the future directions of quantum consciousness research and the potential for groundbreaking discoveries in the field.

One promising area for future research is the study of the relationship between quantum mechanics and consciousness in non-human animals. Most research in quantum consciousness has focused on humans, but it is important to investigate the presence of consciousness in other species. Scientists have already begun to explore this area, with some studies suggesting that certain animals, such as birds and primates, possess an awareness of self and may have some degree of consciousness.

Another promising area of research is the exploration of the connection between quantum mechanics and higher states of consciousness, such as meditation and altered states induced by psychedelics. These states have been shown to have profound effects on the brain, leading to changes in perception, emotion, and behavior. It is possible that the principles of quantum mechanics may play a role in these experiences, and further research in this area could provide valuable insights into the nature of consciousness.

Furthermore, quantum consciousness research can also benefit from advancements in technology, such as brain-computer interfaces (BCIs) and artificial intelligence (AI). BCIs are devices that enable direct communication between the brain and a computer, while AI can analyze vast amounts of data and identify patterns that may not be immediately apparent to human researchers. These technologies can help scientists collect and analyze data related to consciousness and may lead to the development of new theories and models.

Another exciting possibility is the development of quantum computers, which are capable of performing complex calculations at an unprecedented speed. This technology could potentially revolutionize our understanding of consciousness by enabling scientists to simulate the behavior of large-scale quantum systems, such as the brain, and explore the connections between quantum mechanics and consciousness in greater detail.

Finally, the ethical implications of quantum consciousness research must also be considered. As we have seen in Chapter 20, the principles of quantum mechanics have significant implications for ethics, particularly in the areas of medicine and artificial intelligence. Future research in quantum consciousness must be conducted with responsible and ethical considerations in mind, to ensure that the potential benefits of this research are realized without causing harm.

In conclusion, quantum consciousness research has the potential to revolutionize our understanding of consciousness and the universe as a whole. As technology continues to advance, scientists will be able to explore new frontiers in the study of consciousness, from non-human animals to altered states of consciousness to the development of quantum computers. However, it is important to remember that this research must be conducted with ethical considerations in mind, to ensure that the benefits of this research are realized without causing harm. As we continue to delve deeper into the mysteries of consciousness, we can only hope that the answers we discover will lead to a more profound understanding of ourselves and the universe around us.

CHAPTER 21.4: THE ETHICAL IMPLICATIONS OF QUANTUM CONSCIOUSNESS

As we have seen throughout this book, the study of quantum consciousness has the potential to revolutionize our understanding of the nature of consciousness and the world around us. However, with this potential comes a responsibility to consider the ethical implications of this research and its applications.

One of the key ethical implications of quantum consciousness is the impact it could have on our understanding of free will. If consciousness arises from quantum processes that are inherently indeterminate, then it raises questions about the extent to which we are truly in control of our actions. This has implications for legal and moral responsibility, as well as for personal autonomy and self-determination.

Another important ethical consideration is the potential use of quantum consciousness research in developing new technologies, such as brain-computer interfaces and artificial intelligence. While these technologies could have significant benefits, they also raise concerns about privacy, autonomy, and the potential for abuse. For example, brain-computer interfaces could be used to manipulate individuals' thoughts or actions, or to access sensitive personal information.

Furthermore, the study of quantum consciousness raises questions about the relationship between science and spirituality. Some argue that the indeterminacy and interconnectedness implied by quantum mechanics provide a scientific basis for spiritual or mystical experiences. Others argue that such claims are unfounded and potentially dangerous, leading to pseudoscientific beliefs and practices.

In addition to these ethical implications, there are also broader societal and environmental implications of quantum consciousness research. For example, a deeper understanding of the interconnectedness of all things could lead to a greater sense of responsibility for the well-being of the planet and its inhabitants. On the other hand, the development of new technologies could exacerbate existing social and economic inequalities, or contribute to environmental degradation.

Given these complex ethical implications, it is important for researchers in the field of quantum consciousness to approach their work with a sense of responsibility and mindfulness. This includes engaging in open and transparent communication about their findings, as well as considering the potential impact of their research on individuals and society as a whole.

Furthermore, it is important for researchers to engage in interdisciplinary collaborations with ethicists, social scientists, and other stakeholders in order to address these ethical implications and ensure that their work is used in a responsible and beneficial manner. This could involve developing ethical guidelines and principles for the use of quantum consciousness research, as well as engaging in public dialogue and education to promote greater awareness and understanding of these issues.

In conclusion, the study of quantum consciousness has the potential to provide profound insights into the nature of consciousness and reality. However, it is important for researchers in this field to consider the ethical implications of their work and to approach their research with a sense of responsibility and mindfulness. By doing so, we can ensure that this research is used to promote human well-being and the greater good.

FOR FURTHER READING:

1. Albert, D. Z. (1992). Quantum Mechanics and Experience. Cambridge, MA: Harvard University Press.
2. Chalmers, D. J. (1995). Facing Up to the Problem of Consciousness. Journal of Consciousness Studies, 2(3), 200-219.
3. Hameroff, S. R., & Penrose, R. (2014). Consciousness in the universe: A review of the 'Orch OR' theory. Physics of Life Reviews, 11(1), 39-78.
4. Koch, C. (2019). The Feeling of Life Itself: Why Consciousness is Widespread but Can't Be Computed. MIT Press.
5. Penrose, R. (1994). Shadows of the Mind: A Search for the Missing Science of Consciousness. Oxford University Press.
6. Penrose, R. (1999). The Emperor's New Mind: Concerning Computers, Minds, and the Laws of Physics. Oxford University Press.
7. Russell, S. J., & Norvig, P. (2010). Artificial Intelligence: A Modern Approach. Prentice Hall.
8. Tononi, G., & Koch, C. (2015). Consciousness: Here, There but Not Everywhere. In Brain Connectivity (Vol. 5, pp. 1-7).
9. Tegmark, M. (2014). Our Mathematical Universe: My Quest for the Ultimate Nature of Reality. Knopf Doubleday Publishing Group.
10. Wallace, D. (2016). The Emergent Multiverse:

Quantum Theory according to the Everett Interpretation. Oxford University Press.
11. Wigner, E. P. (1961). Remarks on the Mind-Body Question. In The Scientist Speculates (pp. 284-302). Heinemann.
12. Zeilinger, A. (2011). Dance of the Photons: From Einstein to Quantum Teleportation. Farrar, Straus and Giroux.

GLOSSARY OF TERMS FOR "QUANTUM CONSCIOUSNESS"

- Absorption   The process in which a particle takes up energy from an external source.

- Action potential   A brief, electrical signal that passes along the axon of a neuron and causes neurotransmitters to be released from the terminal buttons.

- Action potential   A brief electrical impulse that travels along a neuron's axon and enables communication between neurons.

- Adaptive unconscious   A concept in cognitive psychology that refers to mental processes that occur outside of conscious awareness but that can influence behavior.

- Amplitude   The height of a wave, which represents the strength or intensity of the wave.

- Anthropomorphic fallacy   A common mistake in which non-human phenomena are attributed with human characteristics or traits.

- Antirealism   A philosophical position that denies the existence of an objective reality.

- Arrow of time The asymmetrical nature of time, in which events occur in a particular sequence and do not typically reverse.

- Bell's theorem A theorem in quantum mechanics that states that the outcomes of certain measurements are inherently unpredictable and not due to any hidden variables.

- Bell's theorem A mathematical theorem that shows that certain predictions of quantum mechanics cannot be explained by any local hidden variables theory.

- Brain imaging The use of various techniques to visualize the structure or activity of the brain.

- Brain-computer interface   A device or system that enables direct communication between the brain and a computer or other external device.

- Butterfly effect   The idea that small changes in one part of a system can have significant and unpredictable effects on other parts of the system.

- Causality   The relationship between cause and effect.

- Collapse of the wave function   The process in which a quantum system changes from a superposition of states to a single state as a result of being measured or observed.

- Complementarity The idea that certain properties of quantum objects cannot be measured simultaneously, but only through a complementary relationship.

- Consciousness   The subjective experience of awareness of one's own thoughts, feelings, and surroundings.

- Copenhagen interpretation   One of several interpretations of quantum mechanics that emphasizes the role of the observer in determining the outcome of quantum measurements.

- Decoherence   The process by which a quantum system becomes entangled with its environment, causing the superposition of states to break down and leading to a classical, deterministic outcome.

- Determinism   The philosophical belief that every event is determined by prior causes and that free will is an illusion.

- Double-slit experiment   An experiment in which electrons or photons are fired through two parallel slits, creating an interference pattern that suggests the wave-particle duality of quantum mechanics.

- Emergence   The phenomenon of complex systems or behaviors arising from the interactions of simpler components or processes.

- Entanglement   A phenomenon in which two or more quantum systems become correlated in such a way that their properties are intimately connected, even when separated by great distances.

- Free will   The philosophical belief that individuals have the ability to make choices that are not entirely determined by prior causes.

- Fringe   The pattern of light and dark bands that results from the interference of waves.

- General relativity A theory of gravitation that describes the relationship between space and time.

- Gödel's incompleteness theorem A mathematical theorem that shows that any logical system that is rich enough to include basic arithmetic must be either incomplete or inconsistent.

- Hard problem of consciousness The problem of explaining how and why subjective experiences arise from physical processes in the brain.

- Heisenberg uncertainty principle A fundamental principle of quantum mechanics that states that certain pairs of physical properties, such as position and momentum, cannot both be precisely known at the same time.

- Idealism The philosophical belief that the mind or consciousness is the fundamental basis of reality.

- Indeterminacy The principle in quantum mechanics that certain events or outcomes are inherently unpredictable.

- Interference pattern A pattern of light or matter waves that results from the superposition of two or more waves.

- Local realism The philosophical position that physical properties of objects exist independently of measurement or observation, and that measurements can only reveal pre-existing properties.

- Materialism The philosophical belief that physical matter is the fundamental basis of reality.

- Measurement problem The problem in quantum

mechanics of how to explain the process by which a quantum system changes from a superposition of states to a single state when observed or measured.

- Non-locality   The phenomenon in which entangled quantum systems appear to interact instantaneously, even when separated by great distances.

- Nonlocality   The idea that entangled quantum systems can be correlated in a way that is not explainable by local causes.

- Observer effect   The phenomenon in which the act of observation or measurement affects the system being observed or measured.

- Panpsychism The philosophical belief that consciousness is a fundamental aspect of the universe, present in all matter.

- Paradox   A situation in which a logical argument leads to a contradiction or a situation that seems logically impossible.

- Parallel universes The theoretical concept that there may be multiple universes, each with its own set of physical laws and properties.

- Participation   The idea that the observer plays an active role in the process of measuring or observing a quantum system.

- Philosophy of mind   The branch of philosophy concerned with the nature of consciousness and the mind-body problem.

- Quantum cognition Quantum cognition is a relatively new field of study that applies the principles of quantum mechanics to cognitive psychology. It suggests that human decision-making and reasoning may be better understood by considering the probabilistic and context-dependent nature of quantum systems. Quantum cognition has the potential to shed new light on phenomena such as intuition, creativity, and insight, and may ultimately lead to new approaches for understanding and improving human cognition.

- Quantum mechanics Quantum mechanics is the branch of physics that studies the behavior of matter and energy at the smallest scales, such as atoms and subatomic particles. It is characterized by principles such as superposition, entanglement, and the uncertainty principle, which differ significantly from classical physics. The principles of quantum mechanics have been applied to a wide range of fields, including electronics, materials science, and quantum computing.

- Quantum mysticism Quantum mysticism refers to the use of quantum physics to support mystical or spiritual beliefs. It is often criticized for its lack of scientific rigor and for promoting pseudoscientific or New Age ideas. The principles of quantum mechanics are sometimes used to justify claims such as the power of positive thinking, the existence of psychic abilities, or the role of consciousness in shaping reality.

- Quantum philosophyQuantum philosophy is the study of the philosophical implications of quantum mechanics. It raises questions about the nature of reality, the relationship between mind and matter, and the limitations of scientific knowledge. It has been influential in fields such as metaphysics, epistemology, and ethics.

- Quantum tunneling Quantum tunneling is a phenomenon in quantum mechanics in which a particle can pass through a potential energy barrier, even if it does not have enough energy to overcome the barrier classically. This effect has important implications for the behavior of subatomic particles and has been applied in fields such as electronics and materials science.

- Quantum vacuum   The quantum vacuum refers to the lowest possible energy state of a quantum system, in which all particles are absent. Despite its name, the quantum vacuum is not truly empty, but rather is characterized by virtual particles that spontaneously appear and disappear. The quantum vacuum has been studied in fields such as quantum field theory and cosmology.

- Realism   A philosophical position that asserts the existence of an objective reality independent of human observation or perception.

- Schrödinger's cat Schrödinger's cat is a thought experiment in quantum mechanics proposed by physicist Erwin Schrödinger. It describes a hypothetical cat that is both alive and dead at the same time, due to the principles of superposition and entanglement. The thought experiment is often used to illustrate the counterintuitive nature of quantum mechanics.

- SuperpositionSuperposition is a principle of quantum mechanics in which a particle can exist in multiple states simultaneously. For example, an electron can exist in multiple energy levels around an atom at the same time. This principle has important implications for the behavior of subatomic particles and has been applied in fields such as quantum computing and cryptography.

- Tunneling The quantum mechanical phenomenon in which a particle can pass through a potential barrier that it would not be able to overcome according to classical physics.

- Uncertainty principle   The uncertainty principle is a fundamental principle of quantum mechanics that states that it is impossible to know both the position and momentum of a particle with perfect accuracy. The principle arises from the wave-particle duality of subatomic particles and has important implications for the behavior of quantum systems.

- Wave function   A mathematical function that describes the probability of a particle being in a particular state or location.

- Wave-particle duality   Wave-particle duality is a principle of quantum mechanics that states that subatomic particles can exhibit both wave-like and particle-like behavior, depending on the circumstances of the experiment. For example, electrons can exhibit interference patterns similar to waves, but can also be localized in space like particles. This principle has important implications for the behavior of quantum systems and has been applied in fields such as quantum computing and cryptography.

- Wheeler's delayed-choice experiment   Wheeler's delayed-choice experiment is a thought experiment proposed by physicist John Archibald Wheeler in 1978. It involves a hypothetical experiment where a decision made by the observer at a later point in time can influence the behavior of a photon in the past. The experiment has been interpreted as supporting the concept of retrocausality, where the future can affect the past.

- Zeno effect   The Zeno effect is a quantum phenomenon where frequent measurements of a quantum system can prevent it from evolving. In other words, the act of observation can cause a quantum system to remain in its initial state, which has implications for quantum computing and quantum information processing.

- Zero-point energy   Zero-point energy is the lowest possible energy that a quantum mechanical physical system can possess, even when it is at its lowest possible temperature (known as absolute zero). It arises from the uncertainty principle, which states that there is a minimum amount of energy that any physical system must have, even when it is in its ground state. The zero-point energy has been used to explain phenomena such as the Casimir effect, which is the attraction between two uncharged plates in a vacuum.

ACKNOWLEDGEMENT

Writing a book is never a solitary endeavor, and "Reality Beyond the Veil: Revealing the True Nature of Reality with Quantum Conciseness" is no exception. I am deeply grateful to the following individuals who have supported me throughout this project:

First and foremost, I'd like to thank my family and friends for their unwavering support and encouragement. Your belief in me has been a constant source of inspiration.

I'd also like to express my appreciation to my editor, who provided invaluable guidance and feedback throughout the writing process. Your insights and expertise have been instrumental in shaping this book.

A special thank you also goes out to my colleagues in the field of quantum physics and mind-body medicine, who have inspired me with their groundbreaking research and innovative ideas.

Finally, I'd like to thank the readers of this book for your curiosity and interest in exploring the mind-reality connection at a quantum level. It is my hope that the insights and tools presented in this book will empower you to take control of your life and manifest the future you desire.

With gratitude,

Sai Venkatram

ΔΔΔ

ABOUT THE AUTHOR

The author of the book "Reality Beyond the Veil: Revealing the True Nature of Reality with Quantum Conciseness" is a highly enthusiastic writer Sai Venkatram , who has a background in IT and a passion for exploring the intersection of technology and consciousness.

Venkatram has spent much of his career working in the tech industry. However, he has always had a keen interest in exploring the deeper questions of existence and the nature of consciousness, and he has been an avid reader of philosophy and spirituality for many years.

Venkaram's writing is characterized by his ability to connect complex scientific and philosophical ideas in a way that is accessible and engaging. He has a knack for breaking down complex concepts and explaining them in a way that is both informative and entertaining.

Venkatram's book on "Reality Beyond the Veil: Revealing the True Nature of Reality with Quantum Conciseness"
is the result of years of research and writing on the topic. Drawing on his IT background, he explores the ways in which technology and consciousness are intersecting in new and exciting ways. He delves into the latest research in quantum physics and neuroscience, exploring the connections between quantum mechanics and the human brain.

What sets Venkatram's writing apart is his enthusiasm and passion for the topic. He is genuinely excited about the potential implications of quantum consciousness for our understanding of the universe and our place in it, and this enthusiasm shines through in his writing.

Overall, Venkatram is a highly enthusiastic writer with a background in IT and a deep interest in the nature of consciousness. His book "Reality Beyond the Veil: Revealing the True Nature of Reality with Quantum Conciseness"
is a must-read for anyone interested in the cutting-edge of science, technology, and spirituality, and is sure to be an engaging and thought-provoking read.

EPILOGUE

As we come to the end of this journey through the mind-reality Consciousness at a quantum level, I hope you've gained a deeper understanding of the incredible power that lies within each of us. From the observer effect to entanglement and superposition, we've explored some of the most fascinating concepts in quantum physics and how they relate to our everyday lives.

But the true magic of this book lies in its ability to help you tap into your own potential. By understanding how your thoughts and emotions shape your reality, you can take control of your life and create the future you desire.

Remember, the mind-reality connection isn't just some abstract concept to be studied in a laboratory. It's a real, tangible force that we can all harness to achieve our goals and live more fulfilling lives. By becoming more mindful and intentional, you can create a reality that aligns with your deepest desires.

As you move forward from here, I encourage you to continue exploring the mind-reality connection and all its amazing possibilities. Keep learning, keep growing, and keep manifesting your dreams. And always remember that the power to create your own reality lies within you.

Have you ever had the feeling that there's more to reality than meets the eye? That perhaps there's a deeper, more profound connection between our minds and the world around us than we've been taught to believe? If so, you're not alone.

For centuries, philosophers, scientists, and spiritual leaders have explored the nature of reality and our place within it. But it wasn't until the advent of quantum physics that we began to truly grasp the incredible potential that lies within each of us.

In this book, "Reality Beyond the Veil: Revealing the True Nature of Reality with Quantum Conciseness", we'll dive deep into the mind-reality Consciousness at a quantum level. But don't worry - you don't need to be a physics expert to understand the concepts we'll be exploring. Instead, we'll take an easygoing, down-to-earth approach that will help you grasp even the most complex ideas.

Along the way, we'll explore the fascinating world of quantum physics and how it relates to our everyday lives. We'll discuss the observer effect, entanglement, superposition, and much more. But this book isn't just a science lesson - it's a guide to living a more mindful, intentional life.

By understanding the connection between our thoughts, emotions, and reality, we can take control of our lives and manifest the future we desire. You'll learn practical techniques for harnessing the power of your mind to achieve your goals and create a more fulfilling existence.

So buckle up and get ready to explore the mind-reality connection like never before. Whether you're a quantum enthusiast or a curious newcomer, "Reality Beyond the Veil: Revealing the True Nature of Reality with Quantum Conciseness" will inspire and empower you to unlock your full potential and create the life of your dream

BACK PAGE

Are you ready to unlock the secrets of the mind-reality connection at a quantum level? In "Reality Beyond the Veil: Revealing the True Nature of Reality with Quantum Conciseness" , author Sai Venkatram takes you on a journey through the fascinating world of quantum physics and how it relates to our everyday lives.

Using a down-to-earth approach, this easygoing guide helps you understand complex concepts like the observer effect, entanglement, and superposition. You'll discover how your thoughts and emotions can shape your reality and learn practical techniques to harness this power to achieve your goals.

But "Reality Beyond the Veil: Revealing the True Nature of Reality with Quantum Conciseness"isn't just a book about quantum physics. It's a guide to living a more mindful, intentional life. You'll explore the connection between the mind, body, and spirit and learn how to create a more harmonious and fulfilling existence.

So if you're ready to take control of your reality and unleash your full potential, "Reality Beyond the Veil: Revealing the True Nature of Reality with Quantum Conciseness" is the guide you've been looking for. Whether you're a seasoned quantum enthusiast or a curious newcomer, this book will inspire and empower you to live your best life.

Have you ever had the feeling that there's more to reality than meets the eye? That perhaps there's a deeper, more profound connection between our minds and the world around us than we've been taught to believe? If so, you're not alone.

Venkatram , My Father who created me

Sai , My Father who created my thought

Printed in Great Britain
by Amazon